PRINCESS DIANA

PRINCESS DIANA

A Book of
Questions and Answers

Victoria
Gilvary Nesnick

• • •

M. EVANS AND COMPANY · NEW YORK

Library of Congress Cataloging-in-Publication Data

Nesnick, Victoria Gilvary.

Princess Diana : a book of questions and answers.
1. Diana, Princess of Wales, 1961–   —Miscellanea.
   2. Great Britain—Princes and princesses—Biography.
I. Title.
DA591.A45D535 1988   941.085′092′4 [B]   88-30081

ISBN 0-87131-558-0

M. Evans and Company, Inc.
216 East 49 Street
New York, New York 10017

DESIGN BY BARBARA M. BACHMAN

Manufactured in the United States of America
9 8 7 6 5 4 3 2 1

To all my students who want to know about
Princess Diana

To my lifetime student and daughter, Amy,
who is a princess in her own right

To my sister, Elena, who has always wanted to be
a princess, and still does

To my husband, Bob, a prince amongst men

To my mother, Italia, a queen of hearts

CONTENTS

THE WEDDING OF THE CENTURY

DIANA'S CLOTHES

DIANA'S JEWELRY

PERSONAL INFORMATION

ON BEING A PRINCESS

Acknowledgments

No job is ever completely accomplished alone. Therefore, I would like to acknowledge and thank all those who have helped me accomplish what at times seemed an insurmountable task. Without their help this book would have remained only a manuscript upon my cluttered desk.

Special thanks for photographs go to:
- Robert Archibald, Information Officer, Australian Information Service, New York City
- Nat Boonthanakit, Public Relations Officer, Tourism Authority of Thailand, New York City
- Dallas Chang, Sygma Photos, New York City, for supplying hundreds of slides by the royal photographer, Tim Graham
- Martin Sauber, President, Joe DeFalco, photographer, Glenn Maffei, and especially Janice Ross, "J.R.," of Diversified Photo, Plainview, New York, for their speedy assistance
- Sarah Gardner, Assistant Information Officer, British Embassy, Washington, D.C.
- Gwendolyn M. Gentry, former president of Mississippi's Chapter of the Make-A-Wish Foundation of America
- Peter McInally, Deputy Head, Reference and Library Division, British Information Services, New York City, for his extraordinary help and patience
- Carol McKay, White House Photo Editor, The White House Press Office, Washington, D.C.
- Andrew Phipps, Public Relations Officer, British Tourist Authority, New York City

Appreciation for stamps to:
- Kathleen McGoldrick, Customer Service Representative, Volpone Stamp Company, Hicksville, New York
- Linda Maida, Cash Sales Supervisor, Herrick Stamp Company, Lawrence, New York

Thanks for sharing personal insights to:
- Jonathan Lollar and his mother, Dorothy, of Ocean Springs, Mississippi
- Sally Cooper, Vice President for Media and Public Relations, Make-A-Wish Foundation of America, Phoenix, Arizona
- Andrea Heid, Director of Public Relations, Washington Home and Hospice, Washington, D.C.

Appreciation for editorial assistance to:
- My sister, Elena, for her helpful contributions and encouragement
- Evan Stone and Edward Mansour of M. Evans and Company, Inc., for their technical and professional assistance

Appreciation for professional interest, support, and most of all, faith to:
- Literary Agent, Ruth Wreschner, Authors' Representative, New York
- George C. de Kay, President, M. Evans and Company, Inc., New York

And finally, but by no means least, special appreciation to:
- The exceptional group of people, especially my mother, Italia, who remained my loving family and friends even though I have neglected them in order to accomplish this goal
- Most of all my daughter, Amy Gilvary, and my husband, Robert Nesnick, whose patience, support, and confidence have given me the courage to continue and make my dream come true

DIANA B.C.

(Before Charles)

What is Diana's last name?

D I A N A was given her first name in honor of an eighteenth-century ancestor. She received her middle name, Frances, after her mother. And for her last, she took on her family name of Spencer. This is often referred to as her maiden name, because it remained her last name until she married Prince Charles.

Since Diana's father was the Viscount of Althorp, this meant that Diana was born into a noble family, which made her official name the Honorable Diana Frances Spencer. When Diana was fourteen, her grandfather died and her father then inherited his title and became the Earl of Althorp. Diana's brother then became the Viscount of Althorp and Diana and her sisters received the title of Lady. It was a title Diana rarely used.

Like many people, even Lady Diana had nicknames. As a youngster, her family and the household staff often called her the "Duchess," because she became "ruler" of the nursery and cared for her young brother after "Mummy" left. Diana was known as the "Duchess" because she was always extremely neat, prim and proper, and exceptionally sure of herself. When Diana began dating Prince Charles, the newspapers used to refer to her as "Shy Di," because her school-girlish habit of shyly tilting her head and glancing sideways through her lashes made her appear to be very timid. Lady Diana never liked the nickname "Di." In fact, it is often said that she actually detests it. Even her mother said, "No one in her life ever called her Di." When Diana was addressed this way, she would frequently say, "My name is Diana."

When Diana married Prince Charles, she became known around the world as Princess Diana; but referring to her this way is actually incorrect and unofficial. It would only be proper if she were born a princess. Since she became a princess through marriage, her proper title is "Her Royal Highness, the Princess of Wales," or "Diana, Princess of Wales." Diana is the ninth Princess of Wales and the first person in seventy years to hold that title. She could technically also be called Princess Charles. Diana's other titles are: Duchess of Cornwall, Duchess of Rothesay, Countess of Chester, and Countess of Carrick.

Since she's been a princess, Diana no longer uses a last name. Charles never does either, not even when he was a child. Neither the prince nor the princess have their last name on their passports. When Diana became the Princess of Wales, she assumed Charles's last name, Windsor, which is his mother's last name, and not Mountbatten, that of his father.

Some day Diana's name will change again and probably for the very last time. That will be when Charles finally becomes King of England. He will most likely give Diana the title of Queen, although technically he will not have to do so. If he does, they will then be the King and Queen of the United Kingdom, which is the proper name for Great Britain, which includes England, Scotland, Wales, and Northern Ireland. But at the moment, Princess Diana is actually a Queen-in-waiting. The world is eagerly awaiting the time when Diana will be known throughout the world as Queen Diana of England.

*D*oes Princess Diana have any brothers or sisters?

D I A N A has two older sisters and one younger brother. She would have had an older brother, but he died the day he was born. Her sister, Sarah, who is six years older than Diana, is now married to Neil McCorquodale, who farms in Northamptonshire, England. Her sister, Jane, who is four years older than Diana, is married to Robert Fellowes, the Queen's assistant private secretary. Her brother, Charles, is now Viscount Althorp.

Since Diana's parents' first two children were girls, they wanted their third child to be a boy so that he would carry on the Spencer family name, inherit his father's title, and his enormous wealth; but instead, Diana was born. Even though she was not the boy they had long hoped for, Diana's parents surely loved her just the same. Her father proudly boasts, "She was a delightful child."

*D*oes the princess really have a stepmother?

Y E S, Diana does have a stepmother and her name is Raine. Diana was fifteen years old when her father married for the second time. His new wife was the Countess of Dartmouth. She is the daughter of Barbara Cartland, who has been in the 1987 edition of *The Guiness Book of World Records* for being the top-selling author. (She has written 418 books, which have been printed in seventeen languages and have sold over 400 million copies. Diana has read many of these novels.)

Of her father's four children, Diana was the one who got along best with her stepmother. It took quite a long while before the children finally began to appreciate their new mother. This only happened after Raine was given credit for saving the life of Diana's father. He had suffered a terrible brain hemmorhage and would have probably died if it had not been for Raine's loving care. She sought out the best doctors, hospitals, and medicine, and helped to nurse her husband back to health.

*W*hat type of childhood did Diana have?

T H E first five or six years of Diana's life were happy ones. Her two older sisters showered her with attention, and it's been said that they treated Diana like a live doll. They would carefully bathe and dress her, and then affectionately brush her blond hair. Diana's parents loved their children and also had a nanny, named Judith, to help care for their youngsters. They also had a governess, Gertrude Allen, or "Ally," as she was often called, who taught them schoolwork at home. Diana was taught her lessons as well as how to behave as a proper member of a noble family. She had a strict upbringing and had to follow very specific rules. She was not allowed to be noisy, nor permitted to interrupt while others were talking. At the dinner table, Diana always had to sit up straight and make sure she did not speak with her mouth full of food. She always had to be polite and smile. These rules, which she learned as a child, have certainly helped her in her new role as princess.

Life became difficult for Diana shortly after her sixth birthday. Her mother fell in love with wealthy wallpaper heir Peter Shand Kydd. He was a married man, who had a family of his own. After Diana's mother left her family to start a new life with him, Diana felt her own family life suddenly fall apart. When her parents later were divorced, Diana's father was granted custody of the three children, which meant they stayed with him instead of their mother. It's been said that Diana's mother didn't believe that she was disrupting their lives too much, because she said the children were being cared for by their nursemaids and were already involved in a school routine. She also didn't feel that she was giving up her children because she would still see them at her new home. But in spite of what "Mummy" thought, all three children missed her very much.

That same year other major changes occurred to make Diana feel even more lonely. Her two sisters were sent away to boarding school, and both their nanny and governess also left. Park House, which had always been a lively home filled with loving people, suddenly became a very empty and sad place to live. Diana and her younger brother, Charles, were the only children left in the house, and at first were cared for by their father and their two grandmothers. Although a new nursemaid, Sally, was eventually hired to care for Charles, Diana took it upon herself to mother him. Diana also spent a lot of time playing with her brother, which helped both of them to keep their minds off the fact that "Mummy" had left.

After a while, Diana and Charles started to attend private school. Their father drove them there every day. In the evenings he would spend time with them before bed and listen to all the news of their day at school. He was a very loving father, but because of his upbringing, he didn't show his love with hugs and kisses. Instead, he would greet his children with a handshake. He didn't play with them, but rather simply watched his children at play. He didn't express his emotions and kept most of his feelings to himself. He never talked about his wife, but he did keep pictures of her on his desk and on the mantlepieces. This was a very difficult time for the entire family.

Diana too, like her father, tried her best not to show her feelings, but she was very upset about the fact that her family had broken apart. Somehow she managed to develop a tough personality in order to help her through this trying time. She rarely cried and would always keep herself busy so that she wouldn't have time to think about her family problems. A friend once said that she could always tell when Diana was angry because she would remove all the contents of her dresser drawers and then neatly rearrange everything. Diana probably would have preferred to rearrange her life but that wasn't in her range of possibilities. So instead Diana learned to cope with her shattered life. It's been said that this experience has helped to make her the strong person she is today. As in Diana's case, children from broken homes frequently grow up to be very loving, understanding, and sensitive individuals.

As Diana grew older, she would visit her mother and new stepfather on weekends and holidays at their farm, on a secluded island off the coast of Scotland. During these visits, Diana would fish with her stepfather and look after her mother's Shetland ponies. When the visits ended and Diana and her mother had to say goodbye, "Mummy" tried very hard not to show her sadness, because she did not want to make Diana feel worse about leaving. Although "Mummy" believed that hiding her feelings was the thoughtful thing to do, it robbed Diana of the loving closeness a youngster needs when growing up, especially when parents are divorced. In spite of this, Diana and her mother love one another a great deal. Even today, Diana makes room in her busy schedule to spend time with her mother, who is also her friend.

What kind of child was Diana?

HER father says, "As a baby she could have won any beauty competition." He adds, "She loved her soft toys nearly as much as she loved babies. She always loved babies."

Diana was a remarkably neat little girl, and her governess, "Ally," remembers her as a "tidy soul." Everything in Diana's room, including her toys, was arranged orderly on shelves, and even her closets were in perfect condition.

Ally used to say that Diana was "a real trier," and once saw Diana slide down the staircase on a tea tray. According to a former nanny, Janet Thompson, "Diana wasn't a difficult child, but she could be obstinate. She always knew exactly what she wanted and how she wanted things done. With Diana it was always a battle of wills." Not only did Diana know what she wanted but also exactly what she didn't want to do and how to go about not having to do it. A classmate once reported, "Diana would paint eye shadow on her legs and pretend they were bruises" to get out of certain physical activities at school; but she never missed a class in dancing.

As a teenager Diana was very independent. Although many servants were available to her, Diana chose to wash and iron all her own laundry. She would also wash her sisters' clothes and clean their apartments when she went to visit them. To Diana, cleaning was fun. Now that Diana is a princess, she doesn't have to do any cleaning at all.

When Diana became a young lady, she moved into a London apartment, which the British call a *flat*. Her roommate, Carolyn Pride, said Diana is "someone with whom you could never be bored . . . a very companionable person. I loved her sense of humor. I loved her thoughtfulness and kindness."

Other friends have described Diana as a fun-loving and easy-going person. They say she's always been the considerate type, "the kind of individual who always remembers to send a birthday card." Diana Chamberlain McDonald, who was one of Diana's classmates, once said that Diana "was the sort to help anybody who looked miserable or unhappy. She was always the first to offer a smile."

Where did Diana live when she was a child? Was she really "the girl next door"?

D I A N A was born in a ten-bedroom Victorian mansion called Park House and lived there until she was about fourteen years old. This stone and brick house was originally built for King Edward VII's overflow of guests and staff. It was, and still is today, part of the Sandringham Estate, on which stands the country home of Queen Elizabeth II, Prince Charles's mother. So, for part of each year, Diana was actually "the girl next door," since her home and that of the Queen's were only a few hundred yards apart. Park House overlooks the royal parkland and ballfield, or cricket grounds, as the British say.

Diana always loved Park House, and it's been said this is where she first developed her enjoyment for nature and the outdoors. The sweeping lawns, graced with majestically tall trees, created a perfect playground for the Spencer children. It became even more exciting after Diana's father had an outdoor, heated swimming pool built, fully equipped with a diving board and slide. It was the only pool for miles around, and it was often said that the young royal children from next door, Prince Edward and Prince Andrew (Charles's younger brothers), would come over and swim with Diana and her sisters. In those early days, Charles had always considered Diana a playmate for his younger brother Andrew.

Diana was about fifteen years old when her grandfather died. Her father then became an earl and inherited the fifteen-hundred-acre estate and the Althorp mansion (pronounced "Alltrup"). It was considered "the family seat" because it had been the home of the Spencer ancestors for nearly five hundred years. Moving into Althorp was a sad experience for Diana because she felt she was being uprooted from Park House, where all her fondest memories had been formed. A story has been told that she was so upset by this move that she spent the entire moving-day sitting on a bench eating peaches and talking to her girlfriend, Alex Lloyd.

Althorp was more like living in a museum than a home, for it was full of antique furnishings. There were spectacular sculptures everywhere, and china cabinets overflowed with hundreds of rare porcelain pieces. The walls were lined with magnificient tapestries and priceless paintings, ranking among the best private collections in the world. Elaborate chandeliers hung from its towering molded ceilings. Although it was an exquisite mansion, Diana never loved it the way she had once loved Park House. Today, Diana's father and stepmother still live at Althorp, and parts of it are open for the public to visit.

Diana managed to liven up certain sections of Althorp in spite of all its antiquity. The splendid entrance hall, with its enormous marble floor, was one of Diana's favorite spots. She would set up her record player there and tap dance to her heart's content. Another comfortable spot for Diana was her bedroom. It had two single beds and a sofa, overflowing with the stuffed animals she dearly loved. When Diana was unhappy she would escape into her bedroom, which is one of seventy-five at Althorp, and spend many hours alone reading romantic novels by the world-famous Barbara Cartland, who would eventually become Diana's stepgrandmother. Little did Diana realize, as she read those love stories, that one day she would be living one of the greatest love stories of our century.

When Diana turned eighteen, she inherited a large sum of money from her great-grandmother and used it to buy a three-bedroom apartment in London. A few of Diana's friends roomed with her, shared the rent, and helped with the household chores. One roommate, Virginia Pitman, described Diana's apartment life this way: "She had a lot of friends. A few people came around for supper . . . and she sometimes went to the ballet or the cinema and occasionally out to dinner, but she didn't go out a great deal at night. She liked to stay home and watch the telly and have a very quiet evening . . . We often came back and found her dancing around the flat, just on her own."

What schools did Diana attend?

L I K E many children of noble parents, Diana began her school career at home. At Park House her lessons were taught by Ally, the family governess. Then, when Diana was seven years old, her father would drive her and her little brother, Charles, every day to a nearby private school, called Silfield. Diana attended Silfield for two years, and it has been said that she was a well-mannered youngster. She did not even use the expression "shut-up," because she was taught it was "a swear word." Diana was good at reading and writing. She liked helping out with her brother's nursery class and enjoyed being with the other children at Silfield because it took her mind off the disturbing thoughts of her parents' separation, and eventual divorce.

After Silfield, Diana was sent to live at Riddlesworth Hall Boarding School, a distance of two hours away, which her sisters had also attended. The school was a beautiful mansion, but in the beginning it didn't matter how lovely it was because Diana was very homesick. She rarely got to see her family because the headmistress, Miss Elizabeth Ridsdale, "Riddy," as the girls called her, did not like family members visiting the school, because she wanted the girls to get used to their new routine without any interference. Riddy was friendly but very strict. She would not allow the girls to receive gifts from home, not even birthday presents. Since students were allowed only one piece of candy a day during the week, Diana would gorge herself on weekends with her favorite "cream egg" candy.

Every school morning at 7:30 an old cowbell would awaken the girls, and all one hundred and twenty of them would dress in the same gray skirts, white blouses, and red sweaters. They even wore uniforms on Sundays, which were hats, gloves, and turquoise dresses. After they were all dressed, Diana, along with the other girls with long hair, had to wait in line to have it braided. Diana hated having rubber bands in her hair.

Although she disliked it at first, Diana eventually grew accustomed to Riddlesworth. Teachers appreciated Diana because her work was very neat and she did as she was told. They also liked her because she always volunteered to help others. In fact, she was so helpful during her first year that she won a special award for helpfulness. Diana was an average student. She enjoyed swimming, tennis, and netball, which is similar to American basketball. The part of the school she liked the best was the pet corner. Riddy allowed the girls to take care of their own pets in school because then they wouldn't feel so homesick. Most small pets were acceptable, but birds were not, because one talking parrot had been trained to say "an improper remark." This, of course, made the girls giggle, but made Riddy angry. Diana's pet was a guinea pig she called "Peanuts."

Riddlesworth was just for girls between the ages of seven and thirteen; so, when Diana was old enough, she entered the West Heath Boarding School, just as her sister Jane had done. This school tried to bring out the best features in each girl's character and help to build their self-confidence. Students were encouraged to "develop their own minds and tastes and realize their duties as citizens."

Diana liked West Heath, and especially enjoyed swimming and dancing classes. She won awards in both. She also liked tennis, art, and music.

Diana made many new friends at West Heath, because roommates were changed every semester. Diana and her friends would frequently stay up late at night giggling over the men they would some day marry. It's been reported that Andrew, Prince Charles's brother, was the man Diana had said she hoped to marry one day. Perhaps this is because Prince Andrew was much closer in age to Diana than was Charles. But in spite of what's been said, it was a photograph of Prince Charles and not Prince Andrew that Diana had hanging over her bed. Some people say that Diana never hung up Charles's picture, but that it was a gift to the school from Cecil King, who was one of the school's most generous contributors. Whether it was Charles or Andrew that Diana talked and dreamed about, we all know whose heart she finally won.

West Heath required a great deal of studying, but Diana preferred to read romance novels and watch television instead of studying her schoolwork. She tried to pass the final exams at West Heath twice but was not successful. Her teachers said she was very capable of passing them if she would only exert a little more effort. Diana's father wanted her to stay and try for a third time, but Diana didn't want to, so her mother instead suggested that Diana go to a finishing school in Switzerland. The purpose of a finishing school is to prepare girls for their life in society. Diana went, but she didn't care for it at all because she had trouble adjusting. She had entered in the middle of the school year, so she felt like an outsider. To make matters worse, there was a strict rule that said the girls were only allowed to speak in French and not in English, at all. This was extremely difficult, and Diana couldn't do it. Because she was unsuccessful at French, she felt frustrated and unhappy. She was homesick again, and after just six weeks dropped out of school and refused to return. It's been said that the only thing she had enjoyed in this school was learning how to improve her skiing. But that became very helpful to Diana because it is a sport she now enjoys with Prince Charles.

What type of student was Diana?

D I A N A ' S school records are safely protected from the public, but a few of the people who have worked at her schools have willingly shared their thoughts about Diana's school days. Miss Riddy says, "She was always a decent, kind, and happy little girl. Everyone seemed to like her . . . What stands out in my mind is how awfully sweet she was with the little ones." The principal at West Heath, Ruth Rudge, says Diana was "a perfectly ordinary girl" who wasn't a "goody-goody." She'd hide extra chocolates, talk when the lights were out, and make the other girls giggle at the wrong time. Diana was "a girl who noticed what needed to be done and then did it willingly and cheerfully." When Diana left West Heath, she was presented with a special award for her work on the Voluntary Service Unit. The headmistress explained, "We don't give this every year. It's presented only to outstanding pupils."

While at West Heath Diana had difficulty passing her academic tests. It's been reported that after four years Diana had not passed one of her "O" level exams, which are given to all British students when they're about sixteen years old. The "O" exams are similar to the American academic achievement test and are given in each subject. Once those are passed, students continue in school for two more years and then take an "A," or advanced level, exams, which they must pass before entering college. Diana failed her "O" levels the first time and then retook them, but didn't spend much time studying, so failed them again. In other words, she doesn't have the equivalent of a high school diploma. It's been said that she stayed at school because she had no place else to go and no real purpose to her life. She was very content being herself and didn't want a career. Like many daughters of the rich who aren't interested in college, her parents sent her to a fancy finishing school instead. There, Diana's French teacher said, Diana "wanted to get married and have children of her own."

A friend once said that Diana kept a newsclipping about academic failures who become gifted and successful in life. Diana may not have been the best student in school, but she can certainly be proud of the human qualities and warm personality for which she is remembered. Today, she is considered a success by almost anyone's standard, and it isn't just because she married the Prince of Wales. Diana has made a niche for herself as she intelligently performs the role of a princess, to the delight of the world.

What nationality and religion is Princess Diana?

D I A N A comes from a mixed heritage. She is part Scottish, Irish, English, and American.

Diana is of the Anglican faith. This means she is a member of the Church of England. When Charles becomes king, he will also head the Church of England. It was the fact that Diana and Charles are of the same religion which helped to make their marriage possible.

Is Diana really shy?

W H E N Diana first received world recognition, she was popularly known as "Shy Di," because of the way she tilted her head and glanced sideways. But a palace official, John Haslam, reports, "The fact that she inclines her head on the side is because like so many tall girls, she is aware of her height . . .

not because she's shy . . . 'Shy Di' was never the case. That image was entirely the creation of the press. The Princess has never been shy."

Janet Thompson, Diana's former nanny, adds, "even when Diana was a four-year-old, it wasn't true . . . She always knew exactly what she wanted and how she wanted things done."

Diana's father, Earl Spencer, is basically of the same opinion. Soon after Diana married Prince Charles, the earl said, "Diana always got her own way. I think Charles is learning that now."

But eighty-five-year–old Dorothy Miles who met the princess at the Washington, D.C., Home and Hospice in 1985, has a different opinion. She says, "Princess Diana seemed shy yet very personable and very down to earth."

DIANA
AND
CHARLES

Was Diana really "just a commoner" before she married the prince?

D I A N A was never an "ordinary" person, and even at birth she was far from being "just a commoner." She was born into one of England's oldest and most aristocratic families, which is headed by her father, Edward John Spencer. When Diana was born, Edward Spencer was a viscount, which is a nobleman one step below an earl or count, and one step above a baron. After the death of her grandfather, Diana's father became an earl. It's been reported that Earl Spencer is a "millionaire several times over."

If we trace Diana's family tree back a few hundred years, we find that she is related to three kings: Henry VII, James I, and Charles II. The Stuart kings, of which she is a descendant, was a much grander dynasty than the present-day House of Windsor, of which Prince Charles is a member. Combining their ancestry, the children of Charles and Diana will be descendants from every British ruler. The Windsors and the Spencers are descendants from King Henry VII and his wife, which makes Diana and Charles seventh cousins once removed.

There are even traces of nobility from Diana's mother's side. Diana's great-grandmother, American millionairess Frances Work, was the wife of the third Lord Femoy.

In addition to being related to royalty, Diana is also related to eight U.S. presidents: George Washington (to whom the

Queen Mother is also related), John Adams, John Quincy Adams, Millard Fillmore, Rutherford B. Hayes, Grover Cleveland, Calvin Coolidge, and Franklin D. Roosevelt.

Diana is also related to such celebrities as opera star Enrico Caruso, and film stars Rudolph Valentino, Cary Grant, and Humphrey Bogart. Among Diana's other well-known ancestors are Louisa May Alcott, Amelia Earhart, Margaret Mead, Adlai Stevenson, Lydia Pinkham, Arthur Schlesinger, Jr., Cornelius Vanderbilt II, Gen. George Patton, Samuel Colt, Nelson Rockefeller, "baby doctor" Benjamin Spock, and Noah Webster, of the dictionary world.

Diana's parents have been "connected" to royalty through friendship and position. Diana has known the royal family all of her life. Diana's maternal grandmother (on her mother's side) is a close friend of Charles's grandmother, the Queen Mother. Two of Diana's great-aunts and both her grandmothers were royal ladies-in-waiting, who attended the queen. Diana's father had also been an equerry to both King George VI and the present Queen Elizabeth II (Prince Charles's mother) during her coronation year. (An equerry is the male counterpart or equivalent of a lady-in-waiting.)

Diana's two sisters, Sarah and Jane, have members of the royal family as their godparents, although Diana does not.

With a background such as this, it can never accurately be said that Diana was "just a commoner"!

When did Diana first meet Prince Charles?

N E I T H E R Charles nor Diana remembers exactly when they first met because it was when they were both very young. Charles was twelve years old and Diana was a baby still in diapers. She says, "A lot of nice things happened to me when

I was in nappies." Years passed and it was their next meeting
that has been written down in history as their "real" intro-
duction. Diana's older sister, Sarah, proudly boasts, "I'm Cupid.
I introduced them." It happened in the autumn of 1977, when
Diana was a sweet sixteen and Charles a man of twenty-nine.
Diana was completing her last semester at West Heath, but
had returned to her Althorp home to spend the weekend at
the shooting party her father had arranged. For the first night
there was a grand dinner, and Charles had been invited as
Sarah's guest. The following day was the pheasant shoot, and
this is when the "official" meeting between Charles and Diana
occurred. They were standing in the middle of a plowed field
when Sarah introduced them. Diana was not as physically
striking as she is today, but was instead a slightly plump
teenager with mousy, shoulder-length hair. But her delightful
personality made a strong impression on the prince. It wasn't
until three years later, when they became engaged, that they
publicly shared their feelings of this "first meeting." Charles
recalls Diana as "a bouncy and lively and attractive sixteen-
year-old." Diana says she thought Charles was "pretty amazing." What has become more amazing is that neither one of
them knew it then, but that moment was to be recorded in
history as the first real step of a love story known from one
end of the world to the other.

Where did Charles and Diana go on dates?

BEFORE Diana began to date the prince, she and her sister
were invited to Queen Elizabeth's shooting party in January
1979, at Sandringham. Diana didn't care for "blood sports,"
but it was a special and exciting time because Charles was
there. He found Diana's company refreshing because he could

relax around her. Even the royal family liked her. Diana was also relaxed in their presence, well-mannered, and comfortable with royal formalities.

After that weekend Charles began to "date" Diana. They attended the opera and ballet together. The prince never came to Lady Diana's flat (apartment) nor did he pick her up there because it would have caused too much publicity and commotion. Instead, they met at the theater or wherever they were going.

In July of 1980 Charles twice invited Diana to watch him play polo, and then later they went dancing. She also attended the Goodwood House Ball with him. The prince was beginning to realize that the young school girl he had met in the plowed fields of Sandringham had developed into a charming, beautiful young woman, who was both kind and graceful.

Toward the end of that month, Charles's father, Prince Philip, invited Diana and other guests on board the royal yacht, the *Britannia*. They all watched the boat races during the Cowes Week Regatta. Diana was not paired off with Charles, but she did spend time with him. She even managed to tip his windsurfer and sent him plunging into the cold water of the English Channel. The prince didn't seem to mind it at all. In fact, a week later he sent Diana two dozen roses. She was then invited to join a group at the royal family's Scottish home at Balmoral, and, according to Charles, this was when they both began to "realize there was something in it." They were discovering that their feelings toward one another were turning to love.

Did Prince Charles really date Diana's sister?

Y E S , Prince Charles began dating Diana's oldest sister, Sarah, during the summer of 1977. During that time, the prince also

dated other women; but since he and Lady Sarah were frequently seen in one another's company, the press thought Sarah
was going to be the woman Charles would marry.

At the time they were dating, Sarah was suffering from
anorexia nervosa, a disease which makes people diet irration-
ally, whether they are overweight or not. She was hospitalized
for six weeks, and it is often said that Prince Charles helped
Lady Sarah cure herself.

Although Charles was a very popular bachelor, it was customary for most of his girlfriends not to tell the press anything
about their relationship or dates with the prince. Girls certainly
didn't want to risk any chances of spoiling their friendship
with the man who would one day become a king by publicly
saying the "wrong" thing. But Lady Sarah was different. She
told *Woman's Own,* "Our relationship is strictly platonic. I
think of him as the big brother I never had." Then, in early
1978, while on a ten-day skiing holiday with Charles and
other friends, Sarah talked to the press again. "There's no
chance of my marrying him. I'm not in love with him. I
wouldn't marry anyone I didn't love, whether he were the
dustman or the King of England. If he asked me, I would
turn him down." This statement to the press helped to quickly
end her relationship with Charles. Some time later, Lady Sarah
married Neil McCorquadale, who farms in Northhampton-
shire.

Why did Charles select Diana to be his wife?

E V E R since Charles was a baby, the "prince watchers" of
the world tried to guess who the next King of England would
choose for his bride. When Charles was just four years old,
one magazine published a list of girls, who, when they grew
up, would be eligible to marry the prince. And, as Charles

was growing up, every single girl he dated, especially more than once, was suspected of becoming the next Queen of England. Everyone kept their eyes on "Charlie's girlfriends," because one of them would someday reign with him.

But why did he eventually select Diana to be his bride? There are many reasons. The first, of course, was that he loved her. He found her smile warm and irresistible and her disposition sunny and captivating. He enjoyed her cheerful manner, charming girlish giggle, and wonderful sense of humor. She was beautiful, affectionate, and most importantly a non-demanding friend. Charles said, "You must be good friends and love, I'm sure, will grow out of that friendship."

Not only did he love her but perhaps just as important was the fact that the people loved her also. Her winning personality had captured the hearts of millions. Charles said, "I couldn't have married anyone the British people wouldn't have liked." It was later said that the prince couldn't have married anyone the British people would have liked more. Newsman James Whitaker added, "People had got so fond of her, they'd have turned against him if he'd let her go like all the others."

It was important that the royal family approve of her also, and they certainly did. Lady Diana's social reputation was an unblemished record, which meant that she had never been married before and had no previous steady boyfriends. This was extremely important because the royals did not want to be embarrassed by any romantic stories about the princess, which could some day be sold to the press by a past "lover." This would not have been the proper background for the future Queen of England.

Unfortunately, Diana's parents' reputation was not as spotless. They had gone through a very messy and public divorce, but because attitudes have changed with the times, her parents' history was not taken into consideration to the extent that it would have been some years ago. At one time in English history it would have been unthinkable for a future king to select for his wife a woman of divorced parents. In spite of her parents' history, Diana's ancestors managed to brighten up the picture by the fact that they had included four English kings. A royal bloodline was not required to become the Princess of Wales and future Queen of England, but it just added to the niceties of Diana.

It was also essential to Charles that the woman he selected to be his wife wanted to be a mother too. Charles wanted a family of his own, and especially a son, who would one day inherit the throne. The prince believed that "marriage is a much more important business than falling in love . . . it's all about creating a secure family unit in which to bring up children." And this was Diana's belief also, for she too was eager to start a family.

Charles liked the fact that Diana shared his other interests as well. They both enjoyed music, dancing, skiing, and the outdoors. Diana was also attractive to Charles because she did not smoke, drink, or take drugs. He knew she would set a good example for the nation's youth. She was not divorced nor did she have any strong political affiliations. Charles was quoted once as saying that his choice in a wife should be guided by his head and not his heart. Charles matured enough to coordinate both his head and his heart when he selected Diana for his wife.

Charles needed a woman who was strong enough to handle constant pressure from the press and other critics. She had to be both willing to devote a large part of her life to serving her country and capable of handling all the responsibilities that this entailed. Charles said, "To me, marriage seems to be the biggest and most responsible step to be taken in one's life . . . When you marry in my position, you are going to marry someone who perhaps one day is going to be queen. You have to choose somebody very carefully, I think, who could fill this particular role." Diana was capable of filling that role because she had all the essential ingredients, and whatever she lacked, she could make up for by being a fast learner.

Charles found everything he was looking for in Diana, and what made matters even better was that he found her at the perfect time. He never wanted to rush into marriage, and when he was twenty-seven years old, he had said that thirty would be "about the right age for a chap like me to get married." Although he was a little past thirty when he married Diana, he had sufficient time and experience with other women to know the "right" one when she appeared. Both Diana and Charles were extremely lucky to have found in each other the right person at the right time.

How did Prince Charles propose to Diana?

CHARLES had thought about it for several weeks; and then, on February 5, 1981, five months after they had begun dating, he "popped the question." He had invited Diana to have dinner with him at his Buckingham Palace apartment, and while at the candlelit table for two, he asked, "Will you, could you be my wife?"

Many women would have quickly responded with an excitable "Yes!"; but Charles was not sure that Diana would accept his proposal. Although she was nineteen, she was still considered a teenager and might not have been ready to take on such an enormous responsibility. As the Princess of Wales, and probably the future Queen of England, life would never again be the same for her. She would lose her freedom and privacy, and almost her every word and movement would be made public. There would also be times when lies would be told about her and even written in magazines and newspapers all around the world. It was not going to be a totally glamorous life, because as royalty she would constantly have to be on her

The Prince and Princess of Wales. (Courtesy Central Office of Information, London)

Lady Diana and Prince Charles pose for their official engagement photo at their future Highgrove home. Prince Charles is wearing the uniform of Commander in the Royal Navy. Lady Diana is wearing an emerald green, silk taffeta gown made by Nettie Vogues. Her diamond jewelry was lent to her by Collingwood Jewelers of London, because up to this point she did not own any jewelry elaborate enough for this occasion. (Courtesy Central Office of Information, London)

best behavior. And what could have made the decision even more difficult for the two of them was the fact that once they were married, if it did not work out, they could never get divorced. This is because Charles, as future king, would also be the head of the Church of England, and such a step would not be permitted. Charles and Diana would have to remain married for life.

In spite of the difficulties involved, Diana did not hesitate to say, "Yes!" She was in love for the very first time, very idealistic, and had no doubts that she was making the right decision. She saw the prince as a kind and reassuring individual, and felt that with his help she could conquer anything.

Even though Diana said yes, Charles insisted that she take three weeks to consider her answer so that she could be absolutely sure she wanted to accept his proposal. As he said, he wanted to give her time "to think if it was all going to be too awful."

Diana decided to spend this time with her mother and stepfather at their isolated sheep ranch in Australia. At first Diana managed to have some private thinking time, but it didn't last long, for soon the press was searching for her. When they telephoned Diana's mother to find out if she was there, they were told she wasn't. That was the first and last time Diana's mother said she lied to the press, "but I was determined to have what my daughter and I both knew to be our last holiday together." And she was absolutely right, for within a few days press helicopters equipped with telescopic cameras were surrounding the ranch. They had not been fooled by lies. Press cars were also canvassing the area. At first Diana's exact whereabouts were kept secret by changing the license plates between family and friends. This had the press following the wrong cars. Diana's privacy was being so invaded that her family even stopped answering all phone calls. This, of course, also made it difficult for even Prince Charles to talk with Diana.

He could not get through and was just about to send someone out to look for her; but before he did, someone finally allowed him to speak to the woman he loved.

Diana did not take the full three weeks to make her final decision, but returned to London before it was over. She said she was "thrilled, delighted, blissfully happy" to accept Prince Charles's proposal. On February 24, 1981, the official announcement, by tradition, was hung on the main gates of Buckingham Palace for all to see. Charles was "positively delighted and frankly amazed that Diana is prepared to take me on."

Charles's ship marked the occasion by firing a twenty-one gun salute. Thousands of people around the world sent letters of congratulations and three thousand sent telegrams. Ten thousand engagement presents were received, and there was such an overwhelming delivery of flowers to Buckingham Palace that they filled Charles's apartment to capacity and then poured over into the hallways. Some of the arrangements were taken to Clarence House, where Diana was temporarily staying with the Queen Mother. Others had to be taken to nearby apartments. The world clearly shared in this couple's moment of glory and would continue to follow the lives of these two people for many years to come.

Did Charles ever propose to anyone else before Diana?

P R I N C E Charles was once one of the world's most eligible bachelors. Thousands of women would have loved to marry him, or even be lucky enough to have just one date with the Prince. He had his pick from all the interesting women he met and even from hundreds of those he never met. Mothers from all over the world would send photographs of their daughters to Prince Charles, in hope that he would select one of them to become his bride. It's been reported that Charles kept these pictures in a big candy box and would once a year share them with the men on his staff saying, "And here is the pick of this year's crop."

Charles did propose to one other woman before he proposed to Diana. Her name was Anna Wallace. She was the twenty-five-year-old daughter of a Scottish landowner. Members of Charles's family and friends did not think he had made a wise choice when he asked Anna to be his wife. Although she was very attractive, and even sophisticated, some people felt that she had a temper that would not be suited for a woman who would one day become the Queen of England. Surprisingly enough, Anna did not accept Prince Charles's proposal of marriage. She was not willing to become the Princess of Wales, because it meant that she would have to sacrifice too much of her freedom.

In spite of the fact that she "turned down the Prince," he still continued dating her, perhaps hoping that she would one day change her mind. Charles was a very determined individual, but so was Anna. While on a date with him at the Queen Mother's eightieth birthday party at Windsor Castle, she was annoyed that Charles was not paying enough attention to her. Someone said they overheard her telling Prince Charles, "Don't ever ignore me like that again. I've never been treated so badly in my life. No one treats me like that, not even you." A similar incident happened again the next time they were together, at a ball at Lord Vestey's home. Anna became so angry that she borrowed Lord Vestey's car and drove herself back home to London. This was the very last time Anna dated Prince Charles. A month later she became engaged to, and then married, the Honorable John Hesketh.

D*id Charles actually ask Diana's father permission to marry her?*

A F T E R Prince Charles "popped the question," he called Diana's father to officially ask for her hand in marriage. Earl Spencer says, "They rang me up and Charles said, 'Can I marry your daughter? I have asked her and very surprisingly she said yes.' " Diana's father responded, "I'm delighted for you both." Afterward he jokingly said, "I wonder what he would have said if I'd turned him down." A short time later, Diana's proud Dad added, "She is a giver, not a taker, and that is very rare these days. I think Charles is very lucky to have her."

Before asking Diana herself, Prince Charles was required by law to ask his mother's permission. The prince needed both the queen's and Parliament's (the British government's) official approval before "popping the question" to Diana.

H*ow much did Diana's engagement ring cost?*

D I A N A selected her own engagement ring from a tray the prince had sent to her. She chose an enormous eighteen-karat blue sapphire, surrounded by fourteen diamonds, set in a thin white gold band. Blue sapphires have been a traditional stone for the royal family. The color is often called royal blue. Blue signifies devotion, and hence the expression "true blue." The ring reportedly cost Prince Charles £28,000 (28,000 pounds in British currency). At that time one pound was equal to 2.25 U.S. dollars. This means that if the world famous engagement ring had been paid for in American currency, it would have cost the prince $63,000.

Lady Diana is rightfully proud of her ring and frequently

positions her left hand in such a way that the ring is clearly visible for all to admire and for photographers to capture on film. She does, though, manage to curve her fingertips to conceal the fact that she bites her fingernails. Not even a Princess can be perfect.

Shortly before Diana and Charles were married, Lady Diana was a guest at one of the queen's garden parties. Still thrilled with her ring, Diana shared her excitment with one of the older guests, who unfortunately was blind. Diana permitted the woman to run her fingers across the magnificent stones so that she too could enjoy its beauty. Diana jokingly said, "I'd better not lose this before Wednesday or they won't know who I am."

THE
WEDDING
OF THE
CENTURY

After the wedding ceremony the royal couple rides through the streets of London in their coach. (Courtesy Central Office of Information, London)

Prince Charles and Princess Diana on the balcony of Buckingham Palace. Queen Elizabeth II is at their side. (Courtesy Central Office of Information, London)

How did Diana feel the day before her wedding?

DIANA was, of course, very excited and even nervous as she attended to last minute details before the wedding. She tried to keep herself as calm as possible before the greatest event in her life was about to take place; but it was extremely difficult, because excitement filled the streets of London and celebrations were everywhere. Even children were celebrating. The palace gave them the biggest party in history: 861 tables were set up along Oxford Street and stretched for one and a quarter miles, providing youngsters with soft drinks and hamburgers.

The evening celebration was much more elaborate and included music from many bands and choirs. And then came the largest firework display in two hundred and fifty years, costing about $16,000. The money it raised was used to help one of Charles's charities for disabled individuals. It's been estimated that over two tons of explosives were used to fill the twelve thousand rockets which were fired. The highlight of the evening was the catherine wheel, which spread one hundred feet across the sky. Then the finale delighted everyone, for in the sky appeared the image of Buckingham Palace and Diana and Charles.

Who made Diana's wedding gown and how was it kept a secret until her wedding day?

A husband and wife designer team, David and Elizabeth Emanuel of London, created Diana's wedding gown. The Emanuels knew that the wedding gown would be among the most important and talked about dress not only in the world but for the entire twentieth century. They wanted it to make Diana look like a fairy-tale princess; but before they could start, they needed to know if it had to be bulletproof. Once they learned from Lord Chamberlain's office that it did not, they then proceeded secretly to make the dress. The Emanuels hired a security firm that would protect their shop twenty-four hours a day. Then, as Elizabeth said, "We kept the shade drawn because I've heard that people with telescopes can peer through windows."

They also had a safe installed where they kept all of their drawings, sketches, samples, and designs hidden from all possible "snoopers." But things did not start out simple for David and Elizabeth, because when the safe arrived, it got stuck in the doorway. The Emanuels had to have a crane bring it through the first-floor window. Next they learned that their trash bins were being ransacked and robbed. Everyone wanted to find out what Diana's gown would look like. In order to keep it a secret, the Emanuels no longer continued discarding sketches and fabric scraps but instead burned them at the end of each day; and though they did throw out white pieces of material, none of it was the ivory color that was eventually used. It was publicly said that the Emanuels made several "back-up dresses" just in case the secret "leaked." But then, when the gown was finished, they confessed that there had always only been the one original design.

The Emanuels were successful at keeping Diana's gown a

secret until the world saw it on her wedding day. But four hours after Diana stepped out of her glass coach, a London bridal shop claimed they had made a simple version of her gown. Exactly five hours after that, copies of Diana's fairy-tale wedding gown were on sale to the public. The Ellis Bridal Shop, which makes copies of royal wedding gowns, said they received two hundred orders for gowns just like Diana's.

What was Diana's wedding gown like and how much did it cost?

THE "gown of the century" was made of forty yards of pure silk ivory taffeta and one hundred yards of crinoline netting. Before it was completed, designer David Emanuel had to actually measure the glass coach in which Diana would be riding to make sure that she, the dress, and Charles would all fit. The gown took five months to make, and Diana had to be fitted for it ten different times because she lost fifteen pounds coping with all the prewedding pressures.

The gown had a scooped ruffle neckline and full pouf sleeves gathered at the elbow, accented with a taffeta bow and edged with a cascade of lace. The dress gracefully shimmered from the reflections of thousands of mother-of-pearl sequins and tiny pearls, which had all been patiently sewn on by hand. The twenty-five-foot train was also hand-embroidered and was the longest in the history of English weddings. It looked magnificent against the 652-foot long red carpet of St. Paul's Cathedral. The veil, which also glittered from sparkling sequins, broke the royal bridal tradition because it covered the face of the princess.

Diana's shoes, even though they were hardly seen, were a masterpiece in themselves. They were trimmed with one hundred and fifty pearls and five hundred sequins. The soles were covered with suede and edged in gold to protect her against slipping during her three-and-a-half-minute walk down the aisle. When Diana met Charles at the altar he smiled and whispered, "You look wonderful." Diana replied, "Wonderful for you."

From head to toe Diana was truly presented to the world as a "Fairy-tale Princess." David Emanuel said, "The fairyness was us . . . the regalness was her."

The Emanuels never charged Diana for her wedding gown. They felt the publicity alone was worth a fortune to them. And they were absolutely correct. Their creations are now known worldwide.

The "Wedding Dress of the Century" is now behind glass and is on public display at the Court Dress Museum at Kensington Palace. If you should be lucky enough to see it, remember not to photograph it. Security rules are clearly posted against doing so. But even if you were to try, security alarms would sound and guards would surely be at your side within seconds.

Let's not forget Prince Charles; he, too, was in this wedding. He wore the full-dress uniform of the Commander in the Royal Navy. His valet said dressing Charles was extremely easy because not one new item had to be purchased. "He didn't even so much as need a new pair of socks."

Did Diana follow the bridal tradition of wearing "something old, something new, something borrowed, and something blue"?

THERE are some traditions that most people are extremely reluctant to break, and the bridal tradition is certainly one of them. Every bride wants to begin her new life with as much good luck as possible, including the future Queen of England. Because she was a little superstitious, or perhaps a true romantic, as most brides, Diana, too, followed this tradition very carefully. "Something old" was the Irish style Carrickmacross lace that made up the panels of her gown. This delicate lace had once belonged to Queen Mary. The "something new" was the silk taffeta from which the rest of the wedding gown was made. "Something borrowed" was the Spencer tiara, which held her veil in place, and the diamond-drop earrings that were lent to Diana by her mother. "Something blue" was a tiny bow hidden in the waist band of the gown. And then an extra royal touch was added: a tiny eighteen-karat gold horseshoe, studded with diamonds, which was tucked away into the fold of the taffeta for additional luck. One last step was taken to satisfy another age-old superstition. The last stitch of the wedding gown had to be sewn as Diana was actually wearing it. Speaking of traditions, Diana purposely did not make the customary promise to "obey" her husband.

Was Diana, as most brides, late for her wedding?

I T has been said that Diana wanted to follow this tradition also, but was tricked by the staff of Clarence House, who had put all the clocks ahead while Lady Diana was sleeping. But in spite of this, the expertly-timed wedding procession was still five minutes late because the twenty-five-foot—long train of the wedding gown had to be carefully folded into the snug quarters of the glass coach, and this took longer than had been expected.

What flowers did Diana choose for her wedding bouquet?

DIANA'S bouquet consisted of dainty white orchids and delicate lilies of the valley, gardenias, freesias, and stephanotis. They were framed in leaves of myrtle and veronica taken from bushes planted from Queen Victoria's wedding bouquet of many years ago. Leaves were used from this particular plant because it has been said that Queen Victoria's marriage was one of the happiest Windsor marriages. Golden Mountbatten roses were added to the bridal bouquet in memory of Charles's great-uncle.

Charles had always considered himself Earl Mountbatten's "honorary grandson," because it is said that the earl had a greater influence on Charles's life than any of his teachers or either of his parents. Out of love and respect for the earl, after the wedding, Diana had her bridal bouquet placed in his honor at the Tomb of the Unknown Soldier at Westminster Abbey.

But Diana will always have a copy of her wedding bouquet because she was presented with a porcelain replica of it, after she attended a concert to help the Benjamin Britten Fund for Young Musicians.

Who was in the wedding party?

THERE were two pages and five bridesmaids; all were friends or relatives of Charles and Diana. The boys, eight-year-old Edward van Cutsem and eleven-year-old Lord Nicholas Windsor were dressed in copies of 1863 naval uniforms. The chief bridesmaid was seventeen-year-old Lady Sarah Armstrong Jones, who is the daughter of Princess Margaret. Thirteen-year-old

India Hicks and six-year-old Catherine Cameron are Charles's goddaughters. Sara Jane Gasellee, eleven, is the daughter of Prince Charles's main horse trainer. Her father said, "She's had to keep it a secret at school for two weeks and she was bursting to tell everyone." The youngest bridesmaid was four-year-old Clementine Hambro, who had been one of Diana's kindergarten students and also the great-granddaughter of Britain's former prime minister and wartime leader, Sir Winston Churchill. The girls all wore cream silk dresses, which were simplified versions of Diana's gown. Their sashes and shoes were in yellow in memory of Earl Mountbatten, Prince Charles's godfather, who had been killed three years before by members of the anti-British Irish Republican Army (IRA). The girls all wore fresh flower garlands in their hair, except for Lady Sarah Armstrong-Jones. She wore flower haircombs as her headdress. All the bridesmaids carried small baskets or bouquets of flowers.

Charles did not have one best man. Instead, he had two "supporters": his brothers, twenty-one-year—old Prince Andrew and seventeen-year-old Prince Edward.

Who was invited to the wedding?

T w o thousand five hundred invitations for the church ceremony were sent to family, friends, dignitaries, and other guests. Although this seems like a lot, Diana says, "When you try to spread them out all over the world, it ends up with too few." One hundred and sixty foreign presidents and prime ministers were invited. Among them was President Ronald Reagan, who was unable to attend, but who sent his wife, Nancy, instead, to represent the United States. Kings, presidents, and heads of state from every continent of the world were invited. The kings of Belguim, Bulgaria, Greece, Norway, Rumania, Sweden, and Tonga were invited as were their wives, and so was Queen Beatrix of the Netherlands and the Duke and Duchess of Liechtenstein. Queen Margarethe of Denmark, Princess Grace of Monaco (the former American film star Grace Kelly), the Crown Prince and Princess of Japan, and Sabrina Guinness and Sir Hugh Casson also attended.

The king and queen of Spain refused the wedding invitation and did not attend, because they were angry that Prince Charles and Princess Diana were visiting the Rock of Gibraltar on their honeymoon. Although this area belongs to Great Britain, Spain has long wanted to reclaim it. Even though they didn't attend the wedding, the king and queen of Spain did send the royal couple a wedding present. It was a bronze statue of a horse and polo player, which typifies Charles's favorite sport. When Diana and Charles stopped at Gibraltar, they received a warm welcome from the people there.

Everyone on Charles's payroll plus their wives or girlfriends were invited to the wedding. Flo Moore, who kept Charles's room in order while he was attending Cambridge, was invited and so were Henry and Cora Sands, who often provided Charles with homemade bread during his holidays in Eleuthera.

Diana was given five hundred invitations to invite those of her choice, which included her three former roommates and her old schoolmates and teachers from both Riddlesworth and West Heath. Lady Diana also invited all ten of the people she had worked with at the London kindergarten, some of the staff at Althorp, and her governess, whom she hadn't seen in years. A little American boy by the name of Patrick Robinson attended with his parents, for Diana had taken care of him in 1979 and 1980. Diana also invited twenty-three-year–old Andrew Widowson, who had been crippled from a rugby (football) accident. Two years before that he had been Diana's date at the Oban Ball. Most of the world would have loved to be invited to "the Wedding of the Century," but they had to settle for watching it on television.

Why was their marriage called "the wedding of the century"?

T H E people of Britain were excited that Charles was getting married, because not only had they watched his mother become queen, but they had watched him grow up and take his place in the royal family as well. By marrying Diana, Charles was actually selecting the next Queen of England. In the United States, a president is only elected for a four-year term and occasionally serves a second term. But in England, a king or queen reigns for their lifetime. Watching Charles grow up made the public feel that the prince was an honorary member of every British family. So naturally, they were all delighted to see him get married.

The marriage was also special because of the size of its audience—750 million people witnessed it on television, which rightfully earned it the title of a "Global Happening." It was televised to every continent on earth and was seen in sixty-one different countries and presented in thirty-four different languages, and even captioned for the deaf.

The show continued non-stop for seven and one-half hours on TV and required that seven hundred and fifty miles of cable be set down. There were twenty-one cameras set up in St. Paul's Cathedral alone. The marriage was called "the Wedding of the Century" because it had the largest audience of any wedding in history. American television devoted more time to this than it had for the space shuttle flight or the return of the American hostages from Iran.

The "live" audience was also enormous. Over 600,000 people lined the streets. Most arrived at unusual hours just to ensure that they would see the royal couple as they passed. Stephen Tinsley arrived seventy-two hours early to guarantee himself the perfect spot along the route. Space in front of every office window was sold as a "good seat." The *Sun* had forty reporters equipped with walkie-talkies to provide information for those who were not lucky enough to see it first-hand.

The streets were decorated with four thousand five hundred pots of flowers and fourteen thousand geraniums were planted around the Queen Victoria Memorial in front of Buckingham Palace. As the royal couple drove past, the Strand Palace Hotel released a spray of red rose petals and one thousand doves. The "Wedding of the Century" has been estimated to cost $1 million and was paid for by the queen.

What type of protection was necessary for the wedding?

ALTHOUGH the wedding of the century was viewed by most people as a fairy tale come true, the police saw it as a massive nightmare. For days before, and right up to the wedding day, police with bomb-sniffing dogs had to comb St. Paul's Cathedral, searching for explosive devices. A special crew of police spent the entire wedding day underground in the sewers of London, guarding against the planting of bombs. The crew was nicknamed the "sewer-side squad."

For the actual wedding, nearly four thousand London police, called bobbies, were used to keep order as were mounted police, a commando unit, a riot squad, and a crack C-13 anti-terrorist squad. Hundreds of plain clothesmen were also assigned to "mingle with the crowd." There was a total of seven thousand "protectors" on special duty that day.

On the ground, bobbies were spaced every four steps on both sides of the processional route. Soldiers with fixed bayonets were spaced every six paces. They were ordered to turn away and not look at the royals when they passed but instead keep their eyes on the crowd for anything that looked suspicious. On the rooftops sharpshooting marksmen were stationed along the two-mile span, and in the air a helicopter hovered about and covered an even broader range. And for added security, 131 closed-circuit television cameras monitored the route.

Since before the actual marriage Diana was still technically a "commoner," her security escorts were mounted civil and military police. After the wedding she was protected by a royal guard.

Both Diana and Charles had detectives riding in their coaches disguised as footmen. On the back of Charles's open carriage rode an armed special agent dressed in royal livery. The queen's personal police officer sat near Charles in the cathedral.

Every precaution was taken to avoid any dangerous act, but preparations were in progress just in case an emergency did arise. A helicopter stood ready if needed, and so was a team of top surgeons. Even a supply of blood plasma that matched the royal couple's was supplied in case of some terrible disaster in which it needed to be used.

Ten arrests were made that day in London, but fortunately they all were for minor offenses, such as pickpocketing. As "the wedding of the century" drew to an end that evening, it's been said that "a sigh of relief could be heard for miles around coming from the London headquarters."

Where did Diana and Charles get married?

TRADITIONALLY, England's royal weddings are held in London at Westminster Abbey. But Diana and Charles broke this tradition and were married instead in London's St. Paul's Cathedral. They made this decision for three reasons. First, St. Paul's could accommodate several hundred more people than could the Abbey. And since Diana and Charles had such a long guest list, St. Paul's was a much more comfortable choice. Second, if their wedding had been held in the Abbey, much of the ceremony would not have been seen by the congregation. This is because a screen separates the guests from the choir and clergy. Since both Diana and Charles wanted their wedding to be a total musical and visual experience, they felt it best to be married in St. Paul's. Here the guests and the world-wide television audience would be able to have a complete view of the entire ceremony. Finally, superstition played a role in their decision. Diana's parents had their wedding in Westminster Abbey. Since their marriage ended in a devastating divorce, Diana thought it would be bad luck to start in the same church as did her parents. It was for all three of these reasons that St. Paul's was selected over the customary Westminster Abbey.

Did anything go wrong at the wedding?

T H E royal family, as any family who painstakingly plans a wedding, did not want any "slip-ups." Every conceivable precaution was taken to make sure that this wedding would proceed perfectly, right down to the soles of Diana's wedding slippers, which were carefully made to prevent slipping during her three-and-a-half-minute walk down the aisle of St. Paul's. Even the royal carriage horses were prevented from slipping by scattering sand in front of the cathedral and all along the processional route. But in the end, it was not the horses but the humans who finally "slipped up." The choirmaster was so energetic that he knocked a lampshade over with his baton. At the altar, while Diana was taking her vows, she said Charles's names out of order. She said, "I, Diana

Frances, take thee, Philip Charles Arthur George," instead of "Charles Philip Arthur George." Charles's brother, Prince Andrew, later teasingly said, "She married my father." Although Diana didn't get the names right, she certainly did get the right prince. Later she admitted, "Well, with four names it's quite something to get organized." Prince Charles also made a mistake. He left out one word and changed another. Instead of repeating "All my wordly goods with thee I share," he announced, "All thy goods with thee I share." Afterward, his sister, Princess Anne, jokingly said, "He meant it. It wasn't a mistake at all." In spite of the jokes, it is obvious that even a prince and princess are nervous on their wedding day.

What did Charles and Diana think of their own wedding?

A L L the royal pageantry was new for Diana, who confessed, "I was so nervous . . . I hardly knew what I was doing . . . It was such a long walk up the aisle . . . " But even Charles, who was accustomed to royal fanfares, admitted that he too was a bit nervous, because the size of the celebration was "rather special".

Before the wedding Charles had said that he wanted it to be "a marvelous musical and emotional experience" for all concerned. It was certainly that, for they had three orchestras, a 7,080-piece pipe organ, two choirs, and exquisite soloists. Charles had told Diana that the music must be "stirring, dramatic, and noisy," so you don't "start hearing your ankles cricking." Three months after the wedding Charles remembered the atmosphere as being "electric," and said, "Our wed-

ding was quite extraordinary as far as we were concerned . . .
It would be great fun to do it again."

What does Diana's wedding ring look like?

D I A N A' S wedding ring is a plain, thin gold band. It was
made from the same gold nugget used to make the wedding
rings for the Queen Mother, Queen Elizabeth II, Princess
Margaret, and Princess Anne. This traditional nugget was
found over fifty years ago in a mine in North Wales. Diana's
ring consumed the last portion of this historic piece. The
princess frequently wears the ring on her left hand along with
her sapphire and diamond engagement ring.

What was the wedding cake like?

D I A N A and Charles did not have one but sixteen wedding
cakes, although only one was planned. The other fifteen were
unsolicited, unasked-for gifts.

The "official" wedding cake was four-and-a-half feet high
and weighed two hundred and twenty-four pounds, forty-nine
pounds of which was the white icing. It was a traditional
fruitcake, of which every piece of fruit was individually in-
spected. It required three months to mellow and was baked
by the navy cooks. The largest layer took eight and a half
hours to bake. The major cook, David Avery, said the recipe
is "in my head . . . I first learned it twenty years ago and now
I've added a few things and taken a few things out." The royal
wedding cake was cut using Charles's ceremonial navy sword.
It served one hundred and twenty guests and was estimated
to have cost $6,000.

What did Diana and Charles receive as wedding presents?

SELECTING wedding presents for a prince and princess is not an easy task, but Diana helped her well-wishers by listing three hundred items, any of which she would be pleased to receive. She then gave the list to two London shops so people would have a few suggestions from which to choose. It included items such as a dark green tablecloth, quilted place mats, Royal Worcester china, twenty-four champagne glasses, a spice rack, a pair of white cockatoo statues, fireplace bellows, sun lounges, and a croquet set.

The list proved to be a great success, as Diana remarked, "There was so much coming in, it's very difficult to keep up with it all . . . My list is completely empty. It's all come to us. It's marvelous!" After a moment she added, "But we have two houses to fill." Charles said he had never seen such friendliness and generosity from people as he had since the engagement was announced. "It's incredible . . . incredible kindness. I can't get over it."

It has been estimated that Diana and Charles received more than ten thousand wedding presents. They filled the private movie theater at Buckingham Palace. Every present had to be thoroughly examined by security specialists to make sure that no ill-wishers sent anything dangerous. The gifts ranged from elaborate silver to useful household items. There was even a jeweled mousetrap. Some gifts were extremely expensive, while others were very simple and touching. These came mainly from elderly people and small children.

Stephen P. Barry, Charles's valet at that time, reports, "There were, like any other wedding, some very strange presents. The prince's word for the worst of them was 'frightful!' Then he'd add, 'They can go in the staff rooms.' The staff rooms are now pretty cluttered—mostly with dreadful pictures painted by people who think they're Picasso. There were an awful lot of silver toast racks. 'Can you believe,' he [Charles] said, 'all these toast racks and no one's given us a toaster! Ours must be the only wedding that didn't receive one.' "

The royal couple received a lot of jewelry from rulers of different countries, but the most spectacular present came from Saudi Arabia, which was a stunning sapphire and diamond set for Diana. It contained a bracelet, watch, necklace, pendant, and earrings set in gold and valued at $1 million. Diana said, "Gosh, I'm becoming a very rich lady."

Prince Charles received a large gold box from Saudi Arabia. Stephen P. Barry says, "Charles must have more gold boxes than anyone else in the world . . . It seems to be the only present that people ever think about when they have to buy him something. But then—what do you buy a man who has everything?"

Barry reports, "People sent things from all over the world and extra staff had to be taken on to cope with the unpacking, the categorizing and the thank-you letters." About one thousand presents were put on display for two months at St. James Palace in London, which is a traditional royal custom. Also displayed were Diana's wedding gown and slippers, her bridesmaids' outfits, and the naval uniforms of her pages. Admission was charged, and a sum of £86,000 or approximately $172,000 was raised and donated to a charity for the disabled. Curious people waited in lines stretching over a mile. Some days they stood in the pouring rain just to see the royal couple's wedding gifts.

The following is a partial list of the gifts received:

· Many silver bowls and candlesticks
· A Steuben crystal bowl christened "The Crusaders," from Nancy Reagan, worth $75,000, but which cost her $8,000.

A spokesman for Steuben said, "We offer handsome discounts to the government."

- Four crates of table glass from the president of Italy
- Silver menu holders engraved with the Prince's three-feather emblem on the front and the names of Charles's household staff on the back
- A wooden cove spoon, a bon-bon dish, a silver vase, and sugar tongs, from Prince Charles's former nanny, Helen Lightbody
- A large Royal Worcester bowl from a boy Diana once dated
- Two cases of specially blended "C & D" malt whiskey from the Macallan's Distillery
- A dining-room table made by Prince Margaret's son, Viscount Linley
- A huge stone table from the king of Swaziland
- A complete bedroom set with two extra beds
- Two terry cloth robes embroidered with Charles's and Diana's names, from the youngest bride's maid
- A hand-knitted bedspread made by the queen of Tonga, and a pair of saddles from the king
- A tartan rug from Diana's great-uncle, G. C. Spencer
- Lace cushions from the Royal School of Needlework
- A picnic basket from Lady Anne Wake-Walker
- A Munnings picture of horses, from American oilman, Dr. Armand Hammer
- A seven-foot-high thatched birdhouse
- Western boots for Charles and Western Chaps for Diana, from Texas and Anne Armstrong, the former American ambassador
- A crocodile handbag from the government of Nigeria
- A windsurfer
- Two Jersey cows
- A sheet-iron weather vane, from the villagers of Doughton
- A ball-and-chain paperweight, from the inmates of Dartmoor Prison

- A grand piano
- An herb garden for Highgrove, from the Women's Institute
- A glass wine cooler, from the Automobile Association
- A complete set of fruit trees from the Fruiterers' Company
- A set of garden chairs from the queen and prince of Denmark
- A nickel-silvered mousetrap in a jeweled presentation case, from West Country Councillor, Vernon Gould
- Three hundred uncut multicolored diamonds from Saudi Arabia
- An empty jewel case from Diana's father, which he knew she would surely fill
- A white-gold diamond necklace with a pendant of the three-feathered emblem, from the National Association of Goldsmiths
- A gold choker set with multicolored gems, from the Near East
- An antique Indian piece of jewelry, from the prince and princess of Jordan
- A collage of the fireworks display from the Young England Kindergarten
- A fresh potato shaped like a heart
- A book entitled, *Happiness and How to Find It*
- Diana gave Charles his favorite photograph of her in a green bikini taken on their honeymoon yacht. The frame is gold and studded in diamonds

What were the wedding souvenirs?

I T has been estimated that Britain earned $440 million from the tourists who visited England during the time of the royal wedding and $200 million from selling one thousand six hundred different types of wedding souvenirs. Most of these mementos or keepsakes had painted, printed, or stamped pictures of Diana and Charles. Their faces appeared on everything from teacups to sewing thimbles. Pictures of the Prince and Princess of Wales were also on:

- teaspoons
- drinking glasses
- coffee mugs (one had Charles's face on front with a handle in the shape of one of his large ears)
- dinner plates and place mats
- tea towels
- bed sheets
- clothes hangers
- jigsaw puzzles
- cigarette lighters and ashtrays
- Bibles bound in imitation leather
- postage stamps from more than seventy countries
- replicas of Diana's wedding dress in polyester for under $1,000
- a cannon with Charles's coat of arms, costing $1,200
- a Wedgwood basalt bust statue of Charles, costing $1,700

Although there were souvenirs that cost anywhere from a few dollars to several thousand dollars, many of them could eventually chip, crack, break, tear, or wear out. But one gentleman, Simon Adkins from Cornwall, gave himself a souvenir that would last his lifetime. He had the faces of Diana and Charles tattooed on his back. He had them framed in a heart large enough to add the faces of the royal's children as they were born. Mr. Adkins proudly boasts, "I can carry my devotion to the royal family with me for the rest of my life."

Where did Diana and Charles go on their honeymoon?

AFTER their small wedding reception of 118 close friends

St. Paul's Cathedral, London, site of the "Wedding of the Century."
(Courtesy British Tourist Authority, New York)

The royal yacht *Britannia,* aboard which Prince Charles and Princess Diana cruised the Mediterranean for their honeymoon. (Courtesy British Tourist Authority, New York)

and family members, the royal couple changed into their "going away outfits." Charles put on a gray suit and Diana wore a cantaloupe-colored silk dress with a short-sleeved matching jacket. (A long-sleeved jacket had also been made for her just in case the weather required it.) The princess also wore a matching hat trimmed with an ostrich plume. Adorning her neck was the six-strand pearl choker she borrowed from her sister, Sarah, who had worn it that morning to the wedding ceremony.

As Diana and Charles boarded their open horse-drawn carriage, they were sprinkled with confetti and rose petals for good luck. To the delight of everyone the carriage was decorated with a spray of a dozen silver and blue, heart-shaped helium balloons bearing the Prince of Wales's three-feather emblem. On the back of the landau hung a large "Just Married" sign, decorated with hearts and arrows. It was designed by Charles's brothers with the lipstick they had borrowed from one of the ladies-in-waiting.

The carriage then took the Prince and Princess of Wales to Waterloo Station. Before they boarded the train Diana broke the royal tradition and kissed the two people who had done the most to make her wedding such a success: Sir "Johnnie" Johnson and the Lord Chamberlain. This warm, loving gesture showed the world that the new princess would express her gratitude her own way and not be inhibited by the strict rules of royal protocol.

The royal train then took the honeymoon couple to the Broadlands Estate. This was once the home of Charles's beloved great-uncle, Lord Mountbatten, who had been killed three years earlier by an IRA (Irish Republican Army) bomb. The home is now owned by Mountbatten's grandson, Lord Romsey, who had temporarily moved out to give Diana and Charles their privacy. His home was selected because Charles's parents had begun their honeymoon here and Charles had always hoped that his marriage would be as happy as theirs.

Diana and Charles began their stay by watching the video recording of their wedding. "It's so marvelous to see all the bits you missed," says Charles.

From Broadlands, the couple flew to Gibraltar in an antique but perfectly maintained propeller plane. Prince Charles piloted the plane himself. At Gibraltar they boarded the royal yacht, the *Britannia,* and began their three-week Mediterranean cruise, which had successfully been kept a secret from the press.

The *Britannia,* which was first launched in 1953 and priced at $5.9 million, now cost over $5 million a year just to operate. Many have called it a floating, glittering, blue-jeweled palace. It is fully equipped with a chapel, theater, ballroom, and swimming pool. The sun deck doubles as a launching pad for helicopters and also holds two Rolls Royces for on-shore transportation. In addition, the *Britannia* carries a forty-foot barge, which is used as a ferry; two thirty-five-foot speed boats; two sixteen-foot, fast-moving dinghies; two fourteen-foot sailing dinghies; and a number of life boats.

Most couples are alone on their honeymoon, but Diana and Charles were accompanied by a crew of 276 men and one woman, Diana's dresser. With such a large crew, special precautions had to be taken to ensure the royals' privacy. Before the honeymoon began, all crew members were instructed to leave their photography equipment at home. The only ones on board with cameras were Diana and Charles and their royal photographer. When Diana wanted to go for a private swim, she would enjoy the waters at the bow of the Britannia while the crew swam near the stern. Before Diana and Charles toured the beaches or went ashore for a private picnic lunch, a small crew would first survey the area to make sure it was a secluded spot. Luckily the royals' entire cruise managed to be a secret from annoying press and cameramen.

The Prince and Princess of Wales toured some of the Greek islands, and their final stop was Egypt. There, Diana and

Charles visited President Anwar al-Sadat and his wife, Jihan. Diana enjoyed their company so much that she again broke royal tradition and kissed them both good-bye. Royal protocol states that a princess may only publicly kiss blood-relatives or foreign rulers of equal rank. But Diana followed her heart and not the rules.

Where do Diana and Charles live?

THE Prince and Princess of Wales have two homes. Their "everyday" home is a set of apartments in London called Kensington Palace. Their "weekend" or "country" home is called Highgrove. Neither home was ready when Charles and Diana were first married so they moved into a section of the 602-room Buckingham Palace, which is the home of Charles's parents, Queen Elizabeth II and Prince Philip. This mansion sits on a forty-five-acre park in the center of London and is staffed by a team of three hundred and eighty people. The newlyweds stayed here only a few months while the finishing touches were being done to their Kensington Palace home, which had been badly damaged by fire bombs during World War II. It took five years to renovate or repair and it cost $840,000. It is now cheerfully decorated in shades of pink, green, and beige. The wallpaper in some of the rooms is flocked with Prince Charles's royal, three-feathered emblem. Charles and Diana do not pay "rent" for their Kensington Palace apartments, but will have to pay for any further repairs or changes they might choose to make. The royal couple do, though, pay for their own heating bill. Although this may not sound like much, it has been said that it is a sizable expense since the palace is very drafty.

Kensington Palace is also a family home for other royals and is comprised of many apartments. Number eight and nine make up the private home of Diana and Charles. There are other apartments for Charles's aunt, Princess Margaret, and for Charles's cousins, the Duke and Duchess of Gloucester and the duke's mother, Princess Alice, and the Prince and Princess Michael of Kent. There are also state apartments that are open to the public for about a three-dollar admission charge. Approximately one hundred and fifty thousand people visit it each year. Guards are careful to keep them away from the royal living-quarters. If you should decide to tour it while in London, be sure to tell the cab driver to take you to "K.P.," as it is referred to by the royals. If you should say "Kensington Palace," you will probably be taken by mistake to the hotel that bears the same name.

The two apartments occupied by Charles and Diana consist of twenty-five rooms and spread across three levels, which are easily reached by elevators, called "lifts" by the British. There is a modern kitchen and a special room used just for washing the royal crystal. It contains a wooden sink and drain board to help prevent breakage of the royal dinner ware. There is a wine cellar and two dining rooms, one large enough to seat thirty people. When outdoor cooking is preferred, Charles and Diana go to their roof-top terrace. There, concealed behind a high wall, is a barbeque pit nestled between two chimneys. Charles will frequently cook salmon steaks and corn on the cob. Morning meals are served in the breakfast room, and next to that is a large music room, where Diana takes her morning tap-dancing lessons. There are large reception rooms to entertain guests and private studies for the prince and princess. Diana's is a sitting room with walls lined in family photographs she has taken herself. On the windowsill stands Diana's old school lunch box marked "D. Spencer." This room is where Diana frequently holds meetings with her ladies-in-waiting and her attendants, called equerries. There is a large master bedroom with a four-poster bed, brought from Buckingham Palace. The downstairs bathroom has been decorated by Diana with cartoons of Charles. There is a children's nursery and a separate playroom. An area has also been set aside for the children's nannies, and there are separate living quarters for the staff and domestic help. A floor of Kensington Palace is devoted to offices of all the private secretaries, aides, and ladies-in-waiting.

Outside of Kensigton Palace is a helicopter pad, which provides the royal family with quick transportation when needed. The entire grounds of this home is protected by an infrared beam, which, when crossed, triggers an alarm to alert security men.

The royal couple's country home, Highgrove, is a two-hundred-year–old square Georgian mansion, which sits on 348 acres of open fields and farmland. At the entrance is a beautiful meadow of wildflowers. Highgrove is just two hours away from London, which makes it very convenient for thousands of tourists to go sightseeing there. At first Highgrove was easily seen from the road, and curious camera-clicking people stood around trying to catch a glimpse of the Prince and Princess of Wales. Of course this did not make life very comfortable or private for Diana and Charles. So the people of nearby Tetbury came to their rescue. They presented the royal couple with the perfect wedding gift: an impressive, twenty-foot, hand-wrought iron gate. It was made by a primary school teacher, Maris Cole, and her husband Hector, who taught iron-working at the secondary school nearby. The gate was strategically placed between trees and bushes to keep out unwelcomed visitors and now provides the growing family with the privacy they need. The ornamental gates cost the towns-people $5,000, which they raised by taking up a collection and by selling a souvenir envelope of the couple's wedding day.

Prince Charles had purchased Highgrove before he married Diana, but showed it to her for her approval and help with decorating. Although it cost him almost $2 million, it is small compared to Diana's Althorp home. It has thirty rooms but is

Buckingham Palace, residence of Queen Elizabeth II. (Courtesy British Tourist Authority, New York)   The south front, or King's Gallery Wing, of Kensington Palace, London. (Photo by Victoria Gilvary Nesnick)

Postage stamps issued to commemorate the royal wedding and Princess Diana's twenty-first birthday.

considered a middle-sized house by royal standards. Highgrove has a colonnade porch and a magnificent entry foyer. The rooms are bright and airy and the floors are of highly polished wood. There are nine bedrooms, six bathrooms, four reception rooms, and a small but elegant green dining room. Highgrove also has a billiard room and a large library, which contains the furniture from the apartment Diana had before she married the prince. The halls are coral pink and Diana's sitting room is yellow. There is a nursery wing for the children and domestic quarters for the help: a chef, a butler, the nannies, and detectives. There is also an outdoor, heated swimming pool, which was a gift from the Territorial Soldiers. The princess loves Highgrove because it is a much more comfortable home than her museumlike Althorp house. After spending $1.5 million on renovating and decorating, Diana calls Highgrove "my dream house now." But even the dreams of a princess are tinted with problems and responsibilities. To help provide the needed extra protection, the windows are now bulletproof and walls were knocked down to create a steel-walled inner room to protect the royal family against terrorists. To help make life more convenient for the royals the grounds are equipped with a launching pad where the red royal helicopter can easily fly Diana and Charles off to their engagements.

Although Diana and Charles have two major homes, they also have a house in Scotland and a cottage in the Scilly Isles, which are located off the tip of Cornwall in Southwestern England. They maintain other apartments where they traditionally spend vacations, which they call "holidays," with the rest of the royal family: Christmas at Windsor Castle, New Years at Sandringham, and August at Balmoral Castle in Scotland.

DIANA'S
CLOTHES

How many dresses does Diana own?

I N 1984 it was reported that Diana owned approximately three hundred suits and dresses, of which sixty were ball gowns. By 1988 the number rose to almost five hundred, of which one hundred are ball gowns. Many of Diana's outfits have matching hats, handbags, and shoes, so a special closet is needed for these accessory items alone.

It takes two women working full time to manage Diana's enormous wardrobe. They make sure every outfit is cleaned and properly stored. They also keep accurate records of where and when Diana has worn each outfit so that the princess won't wear the same selection twice to the same place.

When Diana and Charles visited Washington, D.C., in 1985, they traveled with seven thousand pounds of luggage. This is not at all uncommon. On royal tours, Diana's clothes usually fill twenty trunks, while Charles's rarely take more than eight.

How much do Diana's clothes cost?

T H E cost of Diana's clothes has frequently been a "hot" topic of conversation and for newspaper and magazine articles. "Diana

Watchers" around the world all want to know how much the Princess of Wales spends on her wardrobe. Of course, her outfits are paid for in English pounds, but in the equivalent of American dollars, for example, her blue engagement suit cost $484 and was purchased off the rack; in other words, it was not designed especially for her but was bought in a store. When she became a princess, the cost of a typical day dress was $350; her three Walker coatdresses, $950 each; a cocktail dress, $550; and ball gowns were between $2,000 and $10,000. Her black taffeta strapless evening gown cost $1,000. Her shoes cost about $200 per pair; cotton sweaters, $650; matching miniskirts, $100; silk bras, $158 and bikini panties, $118; and a ski suit, $600. The Princess of Wales frequently pays a wholesale price for her clothes, which means that a $1,000 dress will cost the princess only about $400.

There have been many conflicting press reports concerning the actual cost of Diana's clothes. In one year the totals ranged from $40,000 to $250,000. In 1983 reports were that the Princess of Wales spent on average between $2,300 and $3,000 a week. With fifty-two weeks in a year, this meant that Diana, for 1983 alone, spent between $119,600 and $156,000 just on her clothes. Of course, Diana's first few years of being a princess were expensive in terms of clothing because she did not have the type or the number of outfits suitable for royalty. It took a while to establish a wardrobe befitting a princess.

For her two-and-a-half-week tour of Italy in 1985, British newspapers said the Princess of Wales spent between $122,400 and $130,000 for this trip alone. And this was the trip during which Diana received the most criticism for her outfits.

Reports on how much the princess spends on her clothes conflict with one another and few, if any, are accurate because there is a big difference between what Diana's clothes cost and what she actually pays for them. Although reports say her clothes for her Italian trip "cost" about $130,000, it's been reported that the princess only "paid" $31,000. This is because

Her Royal Highness, the Princess of Wales, is sitting in front of a background tapestry at Kensington Palace. She is wearing a long, black velvet evening dress, a pearl bracelet, diamond and pearl drop earrings, and her diamond and sapphire engagement ring. (Courtesy Central Office of Information, London)   The princess does not always wear ball gowns and tiaras, but frequently dresses informally, even when visiting Queen Sirikit of Thailand. (Courtesy Tourism Authority of Thailand)

The princess is wearing a striking silver dress designed especially for her by Bruce Oldfield. She wore it to the 1985 Oldfield fashion show, an annual function to raise money for Dr. Bernardo's Orphanage, where Oldfield grew up. (Courtesy Central Office of Information, London)

Diana, like the rest of the royal family, is entitled to a royal discount on all she buys. This means Diana pays considerably less for her purchases than the public would pay for the same items.

A spokesman for the palace says that Diana, and the rest of the royal family, is very cost-conscious and also very fair. Diana and all the royals make sure that the people who supply them with the things they need will also make a profit on what they sell. Whatever the Princess of Wales actually pays for her clothes is private information known only to Diana, Charles, their royal banker, and the fashion houses.

Some shops refuse to cash Diana's checks, which means that she is actually receiving some of her clothing totally free. This occurs because some designers feel that the "advertising" they receive from the world seeing Diana in their special creations is more than enough payment and that it brings them more money in the way of future business than she could ever pay for the clothes. And they are perfectly right. To illustrate the point, one store sold five hundred copies of Diana's Inca-style sweater in just three days. The manufacturers sold well over one million dollars' worth of Diana's black sheep design sweater. If Diana wears it, people buy it.

*H*ow does Diana feel about being called a "shopaholic"?

BEFORE Diana became the Princess of Wales she did not need a large wardrobe of formal evening gowns nor such a large variety of unique suits and dresses, least of all such a wide selection of hats. But once she became the Princess of Wales, her clothing needs increased tremendously, both in quantity and quality. She attends many social functions each week and frequently one formal evening performance per week. When she's on tour of another country her formal invitations increase tremendously. Therefore she must have an almost inexhaustible supply of elegant clothes for her constant role in front of the public. She must dress to fit the role of a princess and not that of an ordinary woman. She says, "My clothes are for the job." She is constantly representing her country to the rest of the world, so she must always look outstanding. As the London Sunday *Times* once wrote, ". . . a princess is for looking at." People expect a princess to look special, and they would be extremely disappointed if she did not. This was certainly the case when Diana did not dress to the expectations of the people on her tour of Italy. Diana does not want to let people down, but as she said in 1985 to twenty million viewers of Britain's Independent Television Network, "My clothes are not my priority. I enjoy bright colors and my husband likes to see me smart and presentable but fashion is not my thing at all . . . I do think there's too much emphasis on my clothes." Diana is a trend-setter and has single-handedly changed Britain into a multimillion-dollar fashion center of the world. The more Diana spends the more the British market increases.

Who pays for Diana's clothes?

DURING her engagement period Diana bought her own clothes. Stephen P. Barry, Charles's valet during this period, says, "Diana had a splendid time buying a great many new clothes. She bought them with her own money. No bills arrived at the Palace Office and she must have spent a considerable sum, although many of the clothes she wore for photographs were loaned by *Vogue* magazine, which was good for them and good for Diana's pocketbook."

Many people believe that now that Diana is the Princess of

Wales, the British government pays for her clothes. But this is not at all the case. She frequently buys some of her informal outfits from the $20,000 a year allowance she receives from a family trust fund. But Charles pays for the rest of her clothes.

Like other members of the royal family, Diana does not carry cash or credit cards with her. Her detective or lady-in-waiting carries a Duchy of Cornwall American Express Card for whatever the princess buys. Her bills are then received by mail at the palace and are paid for once a month. The Princess of Wales does not have to worry about carrying money nor is she bothered by carrying cumbersome packages. Diana's purchases are either delivered to her at the palace or carried by her detectives.

How does Diana select her clothes?

WHENEVER Diana walks into a room, mouths and eyes open wide. And the question most frequently asked by those who were not fortunate enough to see her is always, "What did she wear?" Her outfits, whether formal or informal, seem to please and excite almost everyone. In fact, although she is now a princess, "The Lady Di" look is still copied by women of all ages. It is no wonder that since she's been the Princess of Wales she has been on the International Best-Dressed List every year except 1987. Clothing manufacturers all over the world are constantly imitating her outfits and sell replicas at a variety of prices. Popular magazines still run articles on how to "Dress Like Dazzling Di for Less." "She does a lot for enabling British fashion to be sold the world over," praises England's prime minister, Margaret Thatcher. Others have called Diana Britain's "Number One Saleswoman."

But reaching this fashion status did not "just happen." Before Diana became a princess she dressed as an ordinary-looking, typical teenager. Although she was always meticuluously about her looks, she did not always dress as fashionably as she does now. She was, though, very aware of the latest fashions because both her sisters had worked for the fashion magazine *Vogue*. Before her engagement, Diana usually wore practical, rather than fashionable, outfits because they best suited her for the outdoor life she preferred. She bought clothes with comfort rather than style in mind. Charles once said, "It was one of the things I always noticed about her before we got married. She had, I thought, a very good sense of style and design."

Before Diana was engaged to the prince she often purchased clothing at Benetton and Harvey Nichols which were among her favorite stores in London. When she became engaged she still frequented the same stores but began to buy more exclusive clothing and shopped with a detective always at her side.

During her engagement period, and even during her princesshood, Diana's clothes would be highly scrutinized by the public, so she appreciated advice from her mother. Later, Diana would consult the top fashion editors of *Vogue* magazine. She's also asked Charles "if this looks right or that looks right, but the chances of turning up in what he says are absolutely nil." When Prince Charles selects one outfit, "I go in the other one," she admits.

Both Queen Elizabeth and the Queen Mother have their own couturier (one who design and makes women's clothes), but Diana does not. Instead of relying on one dressmaker, the Princess of Wales selects her clothes from a variety of designers, all of whom are British. This has certainly boosted Britain's fashion business. Diana either goes to the private showroom of her designers or, more commonly, they visit her at Kensington Palace. They bring sketches and pictures of different outfits as well as small swatches of material so Diana may select the color and fabric of her choice. Donald Campbell, one of

Diana's fashion designers, says, "When I go to the Palace with my fitter to fit five garments, she receives us alone, in the nicest way, and we're in and out of there within an hour. That's not just remarkable, it's doubly remarkable. And I should know. I have my share of difficult customers. Princess Diana is just an ideal customer. She's a delight."

Although Diana does much of her shopping in the comfort of her palace, she will, unlike other members of the royal family, walk into a store, unannounced, to buy things off the rack. One saleswoman says Diana's "very keen on bargains." She is also allowed to shop privately in stores in the morning before they open to the public.

Diana says when she first became a princess, "there were a lot of people to help me. It's now really my own choice, but I can't always wear what I'd like to an engagement because it's just not practical . . . there's always a gale wherever we go . . . and the wind is my enemy . . . and you've got to put your arm up to get some flowers, so you can't have something too revealing, and you can't have hems too short because when you bend over there's six children looking up your skirt . . . Clothes are for the job. They've got to be practical. Sometimes I can be a little outrageous, which is quite nice. Sometimes."

It has often been said that it's the clothes that make a woman outstanding, but in Diana's case it's the woman who makes the clothes outstanding. Thousands of people who have met Diana say that her charming personality outshines whatever she wears.

Even Diana's shoes are a topic of public discussion. Sometimes she buys them already made and sometimes she has them handmade especially for her. When she chooses the latter, she does not have the time to wait and have shoes made to fit exactly, so her shoemaker keeps a carved wooden model of her feet from which he designs and makes her shoes.

How does Diana select the "right" color to wear?

D I A N A tries to select colors that blend with or accent her complexion, hair, and eyes. She always loves bright colors, but never seems to wear bright orange, at least not in public. Aside from this one color, Diana is not afraid to experiment with new shades. She selects bright hues so that she can be seen easily in a crowd and is clearly distinguishable to her bodyguards.

Although she likes vivid colors, Diana has a number of smartly designed black and white outfits, also. But she is rarely seen dressed totally in black. This is because the royal family traditionally wears black when mourning the death of a friend, relative, or public figure. Diana did, though, shock everyone when she wore a stunning black taffeta evening gown during her engagement period. This strapless gown has since been known as "That Dress" and has helped to end the myth of "Shy Di." The Iranian *Time* magazine, which is known for being extremely conservative, printed a photograph of Diana in "That Dress," but felt it was "too revealing," so blackened in her bare shoulders.

When on tour, the Princess of Wales makes an effort to wear the national colors of the country she is visiting. All the outfits she wore in the U.S. were shades of either red, white, or blue. She will also try to please her guests. That is why she wore President Reagan's favorite color, red, when she visited the White House. Diana also bases her color selection on tradition. When she had an audience with the pope, she wore the customary black. For other occasions she will try to wear fashionable colors and will sometimes consult with fashion editors for suggestions.

Often selecting the right color for the princess to wear depends on who else will be attending the same event. It is the duty of her staff to find out what color the people she's meeting will be wearing so that her choice will not clash with theirs. After Diana has then selected her color, her ladies-in-waiting select theirs so they will not clash with the princess.

Diana's clothes come in a wide range of colors and designs and she tries not to wear the same color too often. But whatever the princess wears, she always steals the show.

Does the princess wear a dress only once?

L I K E many movie stars, Diana seems to have an inexhaustible wardrobe. But unlike many Hollywood stars, the Princess of Wales does not wear a dress just once and then cast it aside. She does, though, have some of her old outfits boxed in moth-ball-filled cartons and stored in the cellar of the palace. It's been said that sometimes they are borrowed by Diana's older sister, Lady Sarah McCorquodale. If there is an outfit that the public did not like, Diana might wear it for private dinners at home. Female members of the royal family always wear long dresses for dinner. The princess might also have her "less than popular outfits" remodeled in a different style so they can be worn again more successfully. Diana, as well as the rest of the royal family, has had a number of outfits retrimmed and refashioned. Even her maternity dresses were taken in, altered, and worn again. Charles is also thrifty; he will send his shirts back to the tailor for new cuffs and collars when they become worn and frazzled.

Diana gets a great deal of use out of her clothes, especially the evening gowns, and will wear them with different jewelry to give them a new look. If she wears a suit a second or third time in public, she will change the style of the blouse so the suit then has a totally different effect. Someone once counted and found that for the 109 public appearances Diana made during the first half of 1985, she wore seventy-four different outfits and twenty-seven different hats. Diana certainly does not have a new dress for each occasion. When on her Italian tour, a number of people were a bit disappointed because they had seen some of Diana's clothes before, and they had expected a new fashion show each day. Diana responded, "Well, I'm afraid you're going to see everything time and time again because it fits, it's comfortable and it still works. You know, I feel that a lot of people thought I was going on a fashion tour for two weeks. I wasn't. I was going along to support the British flag, with my husband, as his wife. My clothes were far from my mind."

But Diana's clothes make a lasting impression on people. Three years after Diana visited the Washington, D.C., Home and Hospice, eighty-four-year–old resident Florence Ashlin says, "I remember Princess Diana as a pretty blonde who dresses well."

*W*hy does Diana usually wear a hat?

BEFORE Diana became the Princess of Wales she rarely wore a hat. In fact, when she needed one to wear to a wedding, she borrowed a hat from her sister because she had none of her own. Now that Diana is a princess she owns well over one hundred hats, which cost between $90 and $150. One of the designers who makes her hats, John Boyd, says, now "the Princess likes wearing hats, particularly the small veiled ones . . . She likes happy colors that can be spotted in the crowd."

Diana admits, "Wearing hats gives me confidence." The reason Diana now has so many hats is that English protocol states that royal women must wear a hat to all official daytime functions. Diana certainly attends a great many official events and must have hats to match her various outfits.

At first Diana wasn't particularly pleased with this "rule"

and didn't always wear her hats correctly. In her beginning days as a princess, milliner John Boyd would say, "She didn't always put her hats on properly . . . she would come in and say, 'You must be so cross with me how I put it on yesterday.' But I always told her she was learning fast." Another time he said, "About a quarter of the hats I made for her were worn the wrong way round . . . Now I give her instructions, using lots of arrows to help her get them on right." They help the princess know which brim to curve up and which to turn down. Diana often visits his London shop and lets Boyd know how successful his hats have been.

Mr. Boyd dyes his hats for Diana so they perfectly match the color of her outfits. He also often tints the edges of her veils a deep blue to match her sparkling blue eyes. Boyd, as well as Diana's other six milliners (hat makers for women), must make sure that the hats they design do not hide her face because the public wants to clearly see the princess. The milliners must also make sure that each hat is attractive from all angles and not just from the front. This is because large crowds are constantly looking at her from all sides. Because Diana wears hats so successfully, millions of other women are again beginning to wear them. The British hat industry, which was slowly losing its customers, has since begun to blossom. The thanks have all gone to Diana.

DIANA'S
JEWELRY

Where does Diana get her jewelry? How much does it cost? Is it all real?

B E F O R E Diana married the prince she had very little good jewelry. She owned a simple pearl necklace and earring set, a silver bracelet with hearts, gold stud earrings, a family signet ring, and a three-band, interlocking gold Russian wedding ring. She frequently wore a gold letter *D* on a thin chain. This necklace had been given to her by her classmates at West Heath.

At the time of her engagement, Collingwoods Jewelers of London lent her the elaborate diamond necklace and earring set she had admired, so she could wear it for her official engagement photograph. At first the royal advisors said that Diana could not "borrow" the jewels because royalty were not permitted to do so, but Diana quickly said, "I'm not a Royal yet."

During the engagement period she received one of her most magnificent sets from the Crown Prince of Saudi Arabia. It was made up of matching sapphire and diamond earrings, necklace, pendant, bracelet, and ring. It is worth $1 million. Stephen Barry was Prince Charles's valet at that time and was the one to bring the gift to Princess Diana while she was in Buckingham Palace. He says, "She opened the box, looked at the dazzling jewels with big, startled eyes, and said, 'Gosh, I guess I'm a wealthy lady now!' " Of all Diana's expensive jewelry, she seems to wear this Arabian set the most frequently. She even had a midnight blue velvet dress designed especially to wear with this set.

Since she's been married, all of Diana's fine jewelry have been gifts she has received rather than items she has bought for herself. As a wedding gift she received a diamond and emerald necklace, worth $200,000, from her mother-in-law, the queen, a large sapphire brooch from the Queen Mother, a matching bracelet from Charles, black coral jewelry from the king and queen of Tonga, and an elaborate gold Indian choker studded with multicolored stones from the crown prince and princess of Jordan. She has also received a watch, ring, and cufflinks set in pearls from the emir of Qatar, and a diamond watch from the sheikha of the United Arab Emirates.

The queen has followed tradition and has given Diana the Family Order for being a select member of the royal family. This is a picture of the queen hand-painted on ivory, surrounded by diamonds and worn on a yellow silk ribbon.

Diana now owns pear-shaped diamond earrings with interchangeable centers of sapphires and rubies. Over the years she has received many exquisite sets: a diamond and ruby necklace and earrings set, worth $318,000, from King Fahd of Saudi Arabia; a diamond and sapphire necklace, earrings, and bracelet set from the sultan of Oman; and a $40,000 pair of diamond and pearl earrings from the emir of Qatar. The Princess of Wales also has inherited many pearl necklaces with jeweled clasps, which she can wear either in front or in back. After the first pearl choker was seen on the princess, thousands of women wanted to wear the same thing, so many copies, both expensive and inexpensive, were created to meet the public demand.

When Diana becomes queen, she will inherit from Queen Elizabeth II the world's most valuable private collection of jewels. Diana will some day own twenty tiaras, set with huge gemstones, twenty-seven major necklaces, and more than one hundred gem brooches. In the meanwhile, her mother-in-law, the queen, lends Diana some of this spectacular jewelry to wear at special occasions. In addition to borrowing jewelry from the queen, Diana can also borrow from her parents' Spencer and Fermoy jewel pool. In fact, on Diana's wedding day, she borrowed the three-strand pearl necklace she wore on her honeymoon from her sister Lady Sarah.

Now that Diana is a member of the royal family, she is permitted to accept gifts that are publicly given from heads of state or personal gifts presented privately. One summer afternoon, Diana made the mistake of accepting a diamond ring from a Parisian jeweler, which he presented to her at a polo match. A princess is not allowed to keep such a gift given in this manner, so she arranged for it to be auctioned and gave the proceeds to Birthright. This is one of Diana's favorite charities, which cares for the health of mothers and their babies and funds research into the causes and prevention of birth defects.

Although most of Diana's jewelry is gold and precious gemstones, some of it is just costume jewelry, which she has purchased herself. For example she bought a pair of dangling star earrings for only $39, glittering crescent-shaped earrings for $43, rhinestone teddy bear pins for $75, a bubbling champagne glass pin for $60, and a multicolored rhinestone serpent pin for less than $100. She will sometimes wear inexpensive jewelry mixed with the "real thing," which can easily fool the untrained observer.

What gifts has Diana received from Prince Charles?

B E F O R E they were married Charles would send Diana flowers. Her first "lasting" gift was the expensive engagement ring, an oval sapphire surrounded by fourteen diamonds. Diana was permitted to select the ring herself, and chose this particular one because sapphires are her favorite stones. Before their wedding the prince also presented Lady Diana with an eighteen-karat gold watch and bracelet. The watch is a gold replica of the large, inexpensive leather-strap man's watch that Diana used to wear. The new one is definitely a much more feminine-looking piece of jewelry.

As a wedding present, Charles gave Diana an inch-wide diamond and emerald pendant in the shape of three feathers. It is an heirloom which once belonged to Queen Mary. The three-feather symbol is the coat of arms for the Prince of Wales. When the princess first received it, she wore it dangling from a little velvet ribbon around her neck. Diana would change the color of the ribbon to match her outfits. Now she usually wears it on a diamond necklace, which was given to her by the crown prince of Saudi Arabia. She interchanges the three-feather coat of arms with the sapphire and diamond removable medallion, which originally came on the diamond necklace. Charles has also given Diana a multicolored stick pin as a different version of his three-feathered emblem, as well as an emerald and diamond antique bracelet.

From the prince, Diana has also received a solid-gold powder compact and a ring made from the flawless diamond he had received when he was in Botswana. For Diana's twenty-first birthday Charles gave her a silver mascot of Kermit the Frog for the hood of her Ford Escort.

For Diana's twenty-third birthday Charles gave her a different kind of "diamond." He took her to see a Neil Diamond concert. Diana says, "I've been a fan ever since I saw *The Jazz Singer*." She told the singer, "I wanted to see you in 1977 but my father wouldn't let me. But now he can't tell me what to do." At Charles's request Neil Diamond donated a portion of the show's profits to a trust fund for disadvantaged children.

When Diana's first son, William, was born, Prince Charles presented his wife with a cultured pearl necklace set in diamonds with a diamond heart-shaped locket. Shortly afterward he gave her a gold wire necklace with a gold disk medallion on which he had personally engraved William's name.

Charles has also given Diana a charm bracelet, to which he adds another charm every July 1, Diana's birthday, and at other special occasions. The gold koala bear, which she received as a remembrance of their Australian tour, is one of her favorite charms from Charles, as is the gold wombat, a remembrance of young William's nickname. These charms are rarely, if ever, seen by the public, because they are considered part of the royal family's "personal life."

For Christmas of 1984 Diana received a very unusual gift from her husband. He announced that he was giving up shooting game birds, which is a sport that Diana thoroughly detests. Charles, just to prove how serious his promise was, gave away two of his most valuable guns. Prince Charles certainly tries to please his wife in different ways. He's been known to slip little "surprises" under her pillow at night. Unlike "The Princess and the Pea," Diana finds perfume, jewelry, candy bars, and even love letters before she falls asleep. This may certainly guarantee sweet dreams for Diana.

What gifts has Diana given Prince Charles?

THE Christmas Charles promised Diana that he would give up shooting birds, she promised him that she would start taking horseback riding lessons again. She knows how important it is for the future Queen of England to ride, but has been afraid to do so ever since she was a small child and broke her arm falling off a horse.

Sometime after Diana had received a mascot for her car from

Prince Charles, she gave him a polo pony mascot for his car. Diana also enjoys giving her husband gag gifts. Once she gave him a putty nose and a dark moustache. He had loads of fun surprising the photographers with his "new image." Diana has also given Charles a fountain pen filled with disappearing ink so he could write her secret love letters. For another "fun" present, she gave the Prince a wig to cover his bald spot. Although Charles is a man who has everything, he is missing a few strands of hair. Diana jokingly tried to help him improve his appearance.

How many crowns does Princess Diana have?

D I A N A does not own a single crown but instead two tiaras, which are headpieces with a front but no back. When Lady Diana Spencer married Prince Charles, she wore, for the very first time, the two-hundred-year-old Spencer family tiara, which her two sisters had worn at their weddings. This $1.5 million diamond tiara is a family heirloom, which, according to tradition, should have gone to the oldest Spencer daughter, Sarah, but instead Diana, the youngest, received it. This happened because Diana, as a princess, had a greater need for it and would wear it more often than her two older sisters. Although the Spencer tiara was given to her, it does not actually belong to the princess but instead is loaned to her by the Spencer family.

Diana also received another dazzling tiara as a wedding present from her mother-in-law, Queen Elizabeth II. It was to mark Diana's entrance into the royal family. This, too, is an heirloom, because it had been given to the queen when she was married in 1947, from her grandmother, Queen Mary. It has since then become known as "Granny's" or, the Queen Mary tiara. This was the first royal heirloom that Diana re-

Lady Diana is wearing the gold letter *D* necklace which was given to her by her classmates at West Heath. (Courtesy the British Embassy, Washington, D.C.)

Prince Charles is wearing the full dress uniform of a Commander in the Royal Navy. Princess Diana is wearing a long, cream-colored satin evening dress with matching long-sleeved bolero, diamond and pearl drop earrings, and "Granny's" pearl drop tiara. (Courtesy Central Office of Information, London)

ceived from Charles's family and is worth about $1 million. It is made up of nineteen large, teardrop pearls, suspended from lovers' knots of diamonds. It is mounted on a velvet-covered frame that matches the color of Diana's hair. When the princess wears it, she says it gives her a headache. Diana always takes both tiaras with her on royal tours, but will only wear "Granny's tiara" on especially grand occasions.

PERSONAL

INFORMATION

Is Diana afraid Charles will be assassinated?

A N Y O N E who holds a high position runs the risk of being assassinated. Charles's great-uncle, Lord Mountbatten, was murdered and so was Charles and Diana's friend, Egyptian president Anwar al-Sadat. Sadat had entertained the prince and princess on their honeymoon. When he was murdered, Diana said, "He was just such a special man when he came to see us, and it was so sad because he was doing wonderful things in his country, and one minute he was there and the next minute he wasn't. And that's the awful thing, you can't see them again."

Charles expresses his thoughts concerning Sadat's assassination and possibly his own. "He was a Head of State, which we're not, and he was also a politician and living in the forefront of politics and controversy, which we're not. But obviously there is that awareness that something of that nature could happen, I suppose, to people in our position, and there are those who might want to do something unpleasant. I think you can only be fatalistic, otherwise you would probably go dotty."

As Charles mentions, he is not the most sought-out target, but assassination can come any day to anyone in his position. The thought must always be in the back of his mind and is certainly the main fear of all the bodyguards that constantly accompany him. Even though Charles and Diana seem to have the "perfect life," they are constantly living in the shadow of fear. This has a way of creating a dark cloud over any castle.

How rich is Diana?

"I guess I'm a wealthy lady now," Diana said after she received her million-dollar diamond and sapphire jewelry set from Prince Abdullah. Since then Diana has accumulated many more valuable jewels, which make her a multimillionaire. In addition to these, she shares Charles's total fortune of approximately $680 million, the figure reported in 1988, which has increased considerably from the $450 million it was in 1982.

Charles's income depends solely on the rent he receives from the land he owns in Cornwall. In 1981 it amounted to $1.5 million a year, while in 1988 it doubled, and now reaches $3 million. As heir to the throne he does not pay income tax, but before he was married he returned half of his income to the British Treasury as a goodwill gesture. Now with a growing family, he returns only a quarter of it.

Diana also receives approximately $20,000 a year from her own family's trust fund. Although these figures do not reach the billion-dollar level, being a member of the royal family brings many "fringe benefits." For example, neither Charles nor Diana have to pay for the apartments in which they live. They are only required to pay for the upkeep. These palace apartments, as well as world travel benefits, greatly increase their total fortune.

When is Princess Diana's birthday?

D I A N A ' S birthday is July 1. She was born on this date in 1961 and weighed seven pounds, twelve ounces. Her father, Viscount Althorp, called her "a perfect physical specimen."

One of Diana's most unusual birthday parties was the one she had when she was seven years old. She had been working very hard at school and her father wanted to reward her so, he borrowed Bert the camel from a local zoo, so that all the children at the party could ride it.

For her eighteenth birthday her parents bought Diana a car and helped her pay for a three-bedroom apartment at 60 Coleherne Court, London.

Now that Diana is a princess she celebrates her birthdays quite differently than she has previously. Her twenty-first birthday was a celebration for all to remember. Queen Elizabeth gave permission for seventeen countries to issue a set of four different postage stamps in Diana's honor. Each set contained the country's or Diana's coat of arms, portraits of the princess, and scenes from the royal wedding. These royal stamps went on sale July 1, 1982. Diana and the world will long remember her twenty-first birthday.

As princess, Diana receives hundreds of birthday cards from children all over the world. Some youngsters even send her special pictures they have either painted or drawn. If you decide to send the Princess of Wales a birthday card this July 1, mail it to Buckingham Palace, London, England.

Prince Charles is twelve years older than Diana. He says, "I just feel you're only as old as you think you are . . . Diana will certainly help keep me young."

How tall is Diana and what size is she?

WHEN they are photographed together Charles often appears much taller than Diana, but this is not actually the case. Sometimes Charles is standing on a step higher than Diana, and in one "official engagement photograph," he was standing on a box. Diana will sometimes wear mid-calf length skirts so people won't know she's bending at the knees to appear shorter than Charles. Depending on the source, Diana's height is somewhere between 5'9" and 5' 10¾". One source states that Charles is just a quarter of an inch taller than Diana, but another report says, "in fact, he is marginally the shorter." Whichever report is truly accurate, Diana was certainly very conscious of her height when she first began dating the prince, and tended to slouch a bit to appear shorter than she actually is. This seems to be a common habit of many tall women. After having been a princess for quite a while, Diana now seems more comfortable and proud of her own height and thus her posture now appears much straighter. But she still does not want to tower over the prince, so she is careful to select flat or low-heeled "court shoes," as they are commonly called. Her shoes are size 9½ and are in a variety of colors to match her different outfits. They are usually plain and extremely comfortable for her frequent "walkabouts."

It's often been said that Diana was blessed with a high-fashion model's figure because she is so extremely well proportioned. Designer Campbell says Diana "has a perfect figure. That's why she's so easy to fit." But good figures are not just created at birth but are mainly the result of proper diet and exercise. Almost every morning Diana either swims or exercises for an hour and a half. Before she was married, Diana's weight ranged between 120–125 pounds. In 1981, the year she was engaged, she weighed 133 pounds and wore a size 12 dress.

Now that she is the Princess of Wales, she carefully watches her food intake and tries to maintain her weight at 110 pounds. She now wears a British size 10, which is an American size 8. She is enchantingly graceful in whatever she's wearing.

What *does the princess eat?*

THERE is a royal edict that forbids photographers from taking pictures of the royal family eating or drinking. But in spite of the lack of such pictures, the princess does eat! And a bold photographer or two has actually captured this on film.

Contrary to common belief, the princess does not dine on caviar and champagne. In fact, her meals are quite simple and ordinary. She is very careful about what she eats because she wants to maintain her lovely figure. This is especially difficult because the Princess of Wales has a "sweet tooth" and loves chocolate and a gooey dessert called Bahamian Bananas. Both she and Charles love ice cream. Although Diana enjoys sweets, she will stay away from desserts and have a piece of fruit instead.

Diana tries her best to have three healthy meals a day. She eats light meals and drinks a lot of water. For breakfast she usually has muesli, which is a granola-like cereal, or All-Bran or Special K. The Princess of Wales is an egg lover and will substitute a boiled egg for her cereal. For lunch she usually has a salad, and for dinner she'll have either fish, chicken, veal, or an egg dish. She enjoys yogurt, baked potatoes, and, most of all, baked beans. She rarely has meats such as beef, pork, or lamb because they contain a great deal of fat. Diana and Charles eat quite a bit of vegetables, but as Charles puts it, "I'm not a complete vegetarian . . . I actually find I feel better if I don't eat as much meat . . . It may be that in another ten years time I'll go back to eating meat every day." Diana adds, "Anyway, fish is cheaper." The royal couple go on and off meat and try to stay on a low-fat diet.

When the royal couple entertain dinner guests, they usually serve fresh vegetable soup, followed by salmon, with potatoes and peas. The meal commonly ends with a fruit salad, cheese, and coffee.

The Prince and Princess of Wales have two chefs, who travel between the couple's two homes, Kensington and Highgrove. The couple's young children have their own cooks, who serve them freshly cooked and blended food instead of canned foods.

How does Diana stay so thin?

D I A N A says, "I have an enormous appetite despite what people say." But she doesn't overindulge in the wrong foods. Instead, she follows the queen's advice and eats just "a little of everything." Because she is royalty, if Diana rejects food at a special function, people will say that she's unsociable and insensitive toward the host and hostess. If she eats everything she's served at all her social engagements, she will surely "blow up." Therefore she eats in moderation, which keeps her slim and also polite. Diana says she's faithful to a strict diet so that she does not balloon into the "butterball" she once called herself. Her busy schedule also prevents her from eating too much. She says that while at official functions, "It's impossible to talk and eat at the same time, so you end up chasing a bit of chicken around the plate and then never getting anything yourself. And by the time you get home, certainly there's no time. You're rushing off somewhere else."

Diana says, "I'm not thin; I'm slim. And that's the way my husband likes me." She follows a high-fiber, low-fat diet, but says, "I'm never on what's called a diet. Maybe I'm so scrawny because I exercise so much." She does a disco routine to Diana Ross's album *Work That Body,* and takes dancing lessons, which are a combination of tap, ballet, and jazz. Diana also swims as frequently as she can in the pools of Highgrove, Buckingham Palace, and Windsor Castle. After the birth of her son, William, Diana began following the exercises in Jane Fonda's workout book. It's the exercising on a routine basis that not only helps her look good but feel good as well. Diana's attractiveness is noticed by everyone. Dorothy Miles, a resident of the Washington Home, said that as the princess walked by, Cappy, a cockatiel (parrot), gave Diana "the biggest wolf whistle," which "brought a smile to everyone's face."

Does Diana wear make-up?

A s a kindergarten teacher Diana never used make-up. She never even liked to wear lipstick. But now that she's the Princess of Wales, she is the subject of the world's attention, so must always look prepared. Therefore she accentuates her good looks with a little make-up. She tries to keep it as simple as possible and never "over does it." She has received advice from the experts and has learned how to apply lipstick properly so that it does not smudge or smear. Now she uses soft pinks and corals and will wear a darker red lipstick when it matches her outfits. She wears just a little rouge to give her cheeks more color.

It has been reported that Diana has her eyelashes professionally dyed. She applies a few coats of mascara to make her lashes appear longer and darker, but does not apply anything to her neatly plucked eyebrows. Diana usually uses a soft brown or gray eyeshadow, but will use blue or silver when being photographed. She will use a medium-blue pencil liner on the lower rims of her eyelids to make her blue eyes seem brighter

The Princess of Wales is wearing a dark blue, crushed velvet gown and her diamond and sapphire jewelry. (Courtesy Central Office of Information, London)

The princess is wearing a cossack-style blouse. (Courtesy Central Office of Information, London)

as well as more photogenic. Many people have commented about Diana's eyes. Edna Meiklem, coordinator of the British embassy volunteers at the Washington Home, says, "The princess has the most beautiful eyes that seem to light up her face, especially when she smiles. When she spoke to anyone she looked directly at them, her eyes never leaving their face. I'm sure that others, like me, found it difficult to concentrate fully on what she was saying, being completely overwhelmed by the beauty of her eyes." Diana usually applies her make-up herself, but allows professionals to do it when she is being photographed. The princess uses Neutrogena as a face soap. Her favorite perfume is Diorissimo, by Christian Dior, and her lipstick is made by Clinique.

Does Diana dye her hair?

D I A N A' S hairstyle has frequently been the front-page story on many newspapers and also the cover picture on numerous magazines. It is always in perfect shape, except on her wedding day, when it "wilted." By simply changing her hairstyle the princess actually "stole the show away from the Queen" at the 1984 State Opening of Parliament. At this event the queen wears her crown and full regalia and is always the focus of attention. But when Diana appeared in her new upsweep hairdo, all the cameras were focused on her instead of the queen. Diana's decision to select a new hairstyle for this occasion did not receive much approval from the royal family and she was politely told that her timing was "improper."

Diana's famous layered hairstyle was originally cut by Kevin Shanley. This hairdresser was also cutting Charles's hair for a while. Although people do not try to imitate Charles's style, millions of women across the world asked their beauticians for "The Di Cut."

At the traditional State Opening of Parliament in 1984, Her Majesty Queen Elizabeth II announces the details of her government's policies for the coming year. Many people who had not attended this ceremony previously made sure they were in attendance to see Princess Diana. (Courtesy Central Office of Information, London)

The media have said that Diana's decision to wear a new hairstyle to the 1984 opening of Parliament enabled her to "upstage" the Queen. Diana believed her choice of a more sophisticated hairdo was befitting the occasion. This cream silk organza dress trimmed with lace and satin ribbons was designed by Gina Fratini. The princess has also worn it in New Zealand and Canada. (Courtesy Central Office of Information, London)

In a number of photographs of the princess one can easily see that the roots of her hair are darker than the rest. This, of course, enables people to know that Diana dyes her hair. When asked about this, hairdresser Shanley "spilled the beans" by confessing that the princess "highlights" her hair. Diana would say, "Go on, Kevin, make it a bit lighter this time; you know my husband prefers blondes." Even though it was obvious to everyone that Diana's hair was gradually becoming lighter and lighter, Shanley was still "raked over the coals" for revealing her secret. He was criticized in the British press and also by the British Hairdresser's Federation. Richard Dalton now does Diana's hair.

Before Diana became the Princess of Wales her hair was a mousy, light-brown color and before that had been blonde as a teenager. It is now a golden blonde. The shine is due to regular conditioning treatments and a healthy diet. The princess "highlights" her hair to increase the shine and also because it then photographs better. Having one's hair lightened to look as though it happened naturally by the sun is now popularly called "Di-lights" in Britain.

On one of Diana's walkabouts, she visited a trade school and spoke with a carpenter in training. His hair was cut in a punk rock-style, with a long pigtail dyed red, black, and orange. The princess told him, "It makes a pleasant change to talk about someone else's hair, rather than having everyone talk about mine."

Does Diana smoke or drink?

NEITHER Diana nor Charles smoke, nor do they take drugs. The Prince and Princess of Wales do not like people smoking in their home, either. In fact, visitors who have attempted to smoke in the royal couple's home have reported that when they rest their cigarette on an ashtray it soon disappears. Rumors have it that Charles secretly tosses the butts out the window while Diana tries to conceal her laughter.

It has been said that Diana is practically a teetotaler. She never has an alcoholic drink, but will occasionally take a sip of champagne when a special toast is being presented. Diana will frequently drink mineral water instead of alcohol and Charles will have apple juice. While on their trip to Italy, when most people were drinking wine, Diana was enjoying orange juice.

The Princess of Wales is not only concerned about what she drinks but is equally concerned about what her children drink. She does not allow them to have soft drinks that contain artificial ingredients.

Does the princess watch TV or go to the movies?

W H E N there are no special dinners or glittering balls to attend, the Princess of Wales loves to curl up on a couch and watch TV, while eating scrambled eggs. Her three favorite shows are "Dallas," "Dynasty," and the British soap opera "Crossroads." (Diana had met "Dynasty" star Joan Collins at a fashion gala in 1985. The program was to raise money for Dr. Barnardo's, which is a charitable organization of which Diana is president.) The princess will arrange to have episodes of her favorite programs recorded on video cassette if public engagements prevent her from watching them at the time they are aired. Diana and Charles also enjoy watching the video of their own wedding.

Diana does not allow her children to watch TV shows such as "Miami Vice" and "Starsky and Hutch" because she feels they contain too much violence. Charles also places restrictions on his children's TV watching patterns. He limits the amount of time they can watch TV because he feels that television robs children of any imagination.

One of the privileges of being a member of the royal family is that one does not need to go to the local cinemas to see current movies, but instead can watch them in the privacy and comfort of the palace. Diana and Charles may go to the theater to see the premiere of a particular film, but most times borrow movies from the individual theaters so they can be watched at home. Unfortunately, following the royal "custom" takes some of the fun out of life, especially for young children. So Diana has taken her two sons to the theater to see *Snow White and the Seven Dwarfs*. Diana, too, enjoys going to the cinema and has met with friends to see *Crocodile Dundee*. Even a princess can't follow the rules all the time.

*W*ho are Diana's favorite rock stars?

D I A N A has a number of favorite rock stars and will frequently listen to their albums when she relaxes at home, or on her earphones as she strolls through the royal gardens. The princess enjoys the music of Barry Manilow, Elton John, Phil Collins, Neil Diamond, Lionel Richie, Donna Summer, and Barbra Streisand. She also likes the music of Duran Duran, The Police, Supertramp, Dire Straits, Dr. Feelgood, The Beach Boys, and a Swedish group called Abba.

*D*oes the princess have any hobbies?

T H E Princess of Wales has a great number of hobbies. Some

are quiet and relaxing, such as reading novels. She especially enjoys books by Barbara Cartland, Danielle Steele, and Colleen McCullough. Diana also likes to try her skill at pen and pencil sketching. While on the royal yacht, Diana once did a pencil sketch of her dungaree-dressed son pouting. Afterward she contributed the sketch to help the National Society for Mentally Handicapped Children and Adults. A professional who saw the drawing said, "Either she's a remarkable sort of person or she's had some training in drawing somewhere . . . This shows a talent worth pursuing." Other quiet hobbies of Diana's are embroidering throw-pillows for her home, playing bridge, and collecting china rabbits and owls.

On the more lively side, Diana entertains herself and others by doing her imitation of Miss Piggy, one of the Muppets. Diana also enjoys listening to music and will wear her stereo headset whenever she can. She says, "I'm a great believer in having music wherever I go, whether it's a headset or a radio or a record player. And it's just a big treat to go out for a walk with music still coming out with me." Diana thinks about Charles and then says, "both of us love classical music and the opera and the ballet and go whenever we can." Diana also plays the piano, and "Greensleeves" is one of her specialties. She admits, "I fiddle around; it's nothing to get excited about, but it's marvelous, it's very therapeutic."

The Princess of Wales also enjoys dancing. Before she was married she enchanted the prince at a party by teaching him the basic steps of tap dancing. In 1985 after Diana and Charles attended the White House party in their honor, she excitedly boasted, "I've danced with John Travolta. I've danced with Clint Eastwood. I've danced with Tom Selleck. It was wonderful!" The Princess of Wales keeps in shape by taking exercise classes in tap, ballet, and jazz, which are designed to keep the professionals in shape. She'll take lessons in London, and sometimes watches the London City Ballet rehearsals. Afterward she will sometimes have a cup of coffee from the vending machine and

sit and chat with the dancers about their problems and pleasures. Diana once showed her own dancing skills to a select audience at a Sunday concert at the Royal Opera House. Diana
has a slight dancing problem of her own now. After her son
Harry was born, she developed pains in her back, so now she
must cut back on the number of classes she takes each week.

Diana enjoys outdoor sports also. When they get the chance,
she and Charles will go skiing for a holiday and hope it's not
ruined by hounding pressmen. Diana says, "I love being outdoors . . . I enjoy fishing too and we both do it." Diana also
likes just being a spectator while her husband participates in
his interests. "I enjoy polo enormously," says Diana. "I mean,
I go to as many matches as I can." Charles, a great polo lover,
has been known to play up to six times a week.

Diana is skilled at tennis and plays two mornings a week
at the Vanderbilt Racquet Club. The mornings are set aside
for the couple's routine exercise program. Charles enjoys jog-
ging and Diana enjoys swimming. When her schedule permits,
she tries to swim at least half an hour two or three times a
week. When she uses the queen's glassed-in pool at Buckingham Palace she tries to bring her children with her so they
may play in the walled-in royal garden, which is just outside
the pool area. On weekends, when there is perhaps a little
more leisure time, Diana has been known to swim over thirty
laps. Diana's hobbies certainly help to keep her in good physical shape and also relieve some of the mental pressure that
comes from being the world's most popular princess.

Does Diana have any pets?

HER mother used to say that Diana was fond of "anything
in a small cage." When Diana lived at Park House she had a
ginger cat called Marmalade, and also a gray pony. There were

a lot of pets, especially hamsters, spaniel dogs, and horses. And for extra excitement, Diana would visit the newborn calves on her father's farm. On weekends and holidays she would enjoy the Shetland ponies on her mother's and stepfather's farm.

When Diana was between the ages of seven and twelve, she lived at Riddlesworth Boarding School and, like most other girls, would sometimes become homesick. So "Riddy," who ran the school, allowed each girl to have her own pet, in hopes that this would help cure their homesickness. Here Diana had a tan and white guinea pig she called Peanuts. It had won first prize in the Fur and Feather section of the Sandringham Show.

When Diana married Prince Charles, they received a black Welsh mountain sheep and a black Welsh heifer as a wedding present from the people of Wales. Diana called the cow Sandra.

The prince and princess, for quite some time, had a golden Labrador retriever named Harvey, but he has since grown very old and can't make it up the stairs anymore. He's now at a home in Sandringham with a lot of other dogs. The royal couple then got a Jack Russell terrier they call Tigger.

Of course, the royal couple's children have pets of their own. There are rabbits, and each young prince has his own Shetland pony. William's is named Trigger and Harry's is Smokey. Their indoor "pet" is a rocking horse, a gift from Nancy Reagan. Prince Charles has ten polo ponies, four hunting horses, and another horse used for the steeplechase (a horse race with obstacles). He boards them at Windsor Castle without charge.

Does Princess Diana ride a horse?

"N o," Diana says, "I fell off a horse and lost my nerve." Diana doesn't like to ride horses because once when she was eight years old she was thrown from a horse named Romany. She broke her arm and it took three months to heal. Ever since then she has been afraid to ride again. But recently she promised prince Charles that she would again try to learn how to ride. Diana, who may some day become Queen of England, knows how important it is for a queen to be able to ride a horse. It has been a tradition for years. The queen, who has been riding since she was six, has recently been giving Diana lessons and helping her to overcome her fear of riding horses.

Her Royal Highness is wearing her diamond and sapphire earrings. (Courtesy Central Office of Information, London)

ON
BEING A
PRINCESS

How did Diana learn to be a princess?

THERE is no special school that teaches young ladies how to be princesses. For some it's easier than it was for Diana because they have had a childhood of training. Those who were born princesses learn what they need to know a little each day as they're growing up from their parents and perhaps other princesses. Diana knew quite a bit because she came from a noble family—her father was an earl—but she did not know all that was expected of a princess. There was no planned program to teach Diana all she had to know. She just had to learn as she went along. Charles said, "It's obviously difficult to start with, but you just have to take the plunge." And that is exactly what Diana did when she agreed to marry the Prince. After their engagement was announced, Diana moved into London's Clarence House for a brief time, and it was there that Charles's grandmother, the Queen Mother, helped Diana learn what would be expected from the soon-to-be Princess of Wales. Shortly after that, Diana was given a suite at Buckingham Palace and learned by watching Queen Elizabeth.

Diana said, "I don't think anyone can tell you what's going to happen until you go through the experience yourself." Charles was very patient and "marvelous, oh, a tower of strength," Diana says, with a wide grin and Charles at her side. Charles has been a big help especially with on-the-job training. Diana jokingly says, "My husband's taught me all I know." Diana confesses it was difficult to learn, "purely because there was so much attention on me when I first arrived on the scene and I wanted to get my act together, so to speak, and I had so many people watching me the pressure was enormous. But as years go on it gets better. I'm still learning all the time." Before each engagement there is always much for Diana to learn. She needs to know as much as she can about the person she is meeting as well as the history and significance of the event she will be attending. In this respect, the Princess of Wales is constantly a "student." Her tests come when the important event arrives. We are all her judges. Both the public and the press are quick to give her either a failing or passing mark. Thus far, most of her "performances" have rated a gold star.

*I*s it fun being a princess?

W H E N she first became the Princess of Wales, Diana answered this question by saying, it's "a great challenge . . . It's seventy per cent sheer slog and thirty per cent fantastic." As this indicates, the glamorous life of a princess is not all glittering balls, crowns, and jewels. There are a lot of annoyances that go with the title of Princess because it is a twenty-four-hour-a-day position. Diana, as well as all members of the royal family, is always on parade with the world as her constant audience. One of her classmates once said that Diana's life was like walking a tightrope in a circus. Diana can no longer enjoy the simple pleasures of life, such as walking down the street or privately enjoying a shopping spree. Wherever she goes people flock around her and traffic jams are created. And many of her onlookers are extremely critical. While at a party, Diana once confessed to an editor that she "can't do anything right.

If I go to Harrods and come out with a box of something, the waiting photographers want to know what I bought. And if I tell them, they'll print that I spent two thousand pounds. And if I don't tell them, they'll print that I spent two thousand pounds on clothes. And if I come out without anything, they'll print that I went into Harrods for a half hour and didn't buy a thing. You just can't win."

Being a princess means that Diana must always follow the rules or "protocol," as they're called. These rules let her know how to act, how to talk, and how to look in public. For example, she is not supposed to chew gum or use "bad" words in public. She must always look her best and never wear jeans to a public event. She learned a lot of these rules from the royal family, and once said, "With Prince Charles beside me I can't go wrong." But right before her twenty-second birthday, when she was in Canada, she confessed to Newfoundland's Premier Peckford, "I am finding it very difficult to cope with the pressures of being the Princess of Wales, but I am learning to cope with it. I have learned a lot in the last few months . . . and I feel I am doing my job better now than I was before. I have matured a lot recently and got used to coping with things."

Diana must always be polite and can never again behave in a silly, schoolgirlish fashion. She must always behave in a manner befitting a princess and the future Queen of England. Diana jokingly said, "I think that's probably just as well—if you knew how I used to behave."

One of the most difficult rules the princess must follow is that of not revealing strong emotions in public. As a royal she must maintain her composure constantly and not allow her annoyance, anger, or frustration to be seen by the public. She must keep many of her true feelings to herself and not openly share them with others. This is because she will certainly be quoted and publicized around the world, as was her famous expression of displeasure, "Yuk."

Another simple pleasure that most of us take for granted, but which a princess cannot, is that of sharing personal secrets. Diana, as well as all the royals, must be extremely careful about what she says and to whom she says it. Sometimes confiding in a friend can create the "leak" that journalists turn into monumental news items. Newspapers have been known to pay large sums of money for a "juicy news scoop" about the princess and her family. This can make it difficult for even the closest friend to keep a secret. Diana must constantly guard personal information from friends and even her household help.

Sometimes "gossip" manages to leak out and inaccurate rumors are given to the press, but it has been the tradition of the royal family not to reply to criticism or defend itself to the public. Diana says, "You've got to push yourself out and remember that some people, hopefully, don't believe everything they read about you." She adds, "When they write something horrible, I get a horrible feeling right here," as she points to her heart, "and I don't want to go outside . . . It will probably take five or ten years for me to get used to it."

Another "problem" that comes with being a princess is, one which all other working women with children encounter: mothers who work outside the home cannot spend as much time with their children as they would like. One of Diana's biggest disappointments was that she could not be with her son on his first birthday because she was on tour in Canada with Prince Charles. She sadly said, "I wish I had William with me. I miss him very much."

Being a princess has many good points, and one of them is the feeling of being loved by most of the world. And along with that come some "fringe benefits." People often display their love by presenting their loved ones with presents. Diana and Charles have certainly been showered with gifts. When they visited Australia, they received approximately one thousand five hundred presents a day. By the end of the week that amounted to a grand total of 52,500 gifts. Over 140 of them were the country's typical boomerangs and 250 stuffed koala bears for young William. Charles received almost a lifetime supply of the honey he so much enjoys. The royal couple donated most of these gifts to hospitals and orphanages but each and every gift giver, within three days, received a royal thank-you note. Even though many of the gifts were not kept, they definitely created an overwhelming display of love that certainly helps Diana to look on the bright side of being a princess.

Did Diana have to give up her old friends when she became a princess?

BEFORE Diana became a princess, her best friends were her three roommates, and the group used to call themselves the Four Musketeers. The day Diana became engaged to the prince, she moved out of her flat but left her roommates her new unlisted telephone number with a note that read, "For God's sake, ring me up . . . I'm going to need you." The three girls were invited to the wedding, and Diana saw them frequently after she was married. She'd either meet them outside the palace, or "I sometimes have my friends to lunch if my husband's out." Diana would also invite her friends over for casual teas. Virginia Pitman, who was one of Diana's roommates, is presently involved with her art career, and Carolyn Pride is now married to a disco manager and heir to a brewery fortune. Anne Bolton, a third roommate, is also married and is living in Australia. Diana keeps in contact with all three of her past "flatmates."

Charles's valet, Stephen P. Barry, reports that for the first few months, "She kept up with most of the people she dealt with before she became a member of the royal family. The only ones she cut off have been the Emanuels, who made her wedding dress. They got carried away and talked too much to too many people. 'We'll see about them,' said the princess, which meant that she didn't see them again." Members of the royal family have to be very careful about whom they talk to and who they select as friends. The moment a "friend" tells the public or the press a royal secret is usually the moment that person stops being a friend of the royal family.

Since she's been the Princess of Wales, Diana has made new friends. She likes Catherine Soames, who was one of her brides-maids, and also Carolyn Herbert, who is the daughter of the queen's racing manager. Carolyn looks a great deal like Diana, and it's been said that she will sometimes act as a decoy when Diana wants to avoid large crowds. The press has reported that another of Diana's friends is Lady Penelope Romsey, who at "one time had a long romantic relationship with Charles." She is now married and has two children of her own. Lady Penelope was extremely helpful to Diana when she was first learning how to cope with the pressures of being a princess.

Anne Beckwith-Smith, Diana's full-time lady-in-waiting is also one of the princess's closest friends. She frequently sits at the table with Diana and Charles while they're having dinner. Diana calls her "darling" and treats her more like a sister than a lady-in-waiting.

Diana is also very good friends with "Fergie" (Sarah Ferguson), Prince Andrew's wife. In fact, Sarah, the Duchess of York, was the only guest, outside the royal family, invited to Diana's twenty-first birthday luncheon at Kensington Palace. Diana and Fergie, who are fourth cousins, have been friends for a long time and are now sisters-in-law. They spend a lot of time together and share clothes and jewelry.

How does Diana feel about being photographed?

M A N Y people feel complimented when someone wants to take their picture. But such compliments can quickly become annoying if hundreds of people are constantly setting off flash bulbs in front of your face and trying to photograph your each and every move. Before Diana was engaged to Prince Charles, she received no protection at all from the royal palace against photographers. They staked out the kindergarten at which she worked and also her flat (apartment), just to get a snapshot of "Prince Charles's new girlfriend." They even chased after her in their high-speed cars and followed her red Mini-Metro wherever she went. Diana's private life was private no longer. Once, after constant badgering by the press, Diana broke down in tears. Even a princess is human and resorts to expressing human emotions when frustrated beyond her limit. The newsman soon regretted his behavior and tried to make amends by thoughtfully slipping a note onto the front seat of Diana's car, which said, "We didn't mean this to happen. Our full apologies."

When Diana became engaged to the prince things got even worse. Hordes of press cars then followed her, and photographers hounded her daily. Everyone wanted a picture of the soon-to-be Princess of Wales, who would possibly become the future Queen of England. Even though she was constantly hounded by the press, most of the time she managed to tolerate them and even was able to do so with a smile. She once told Charles, "I love working with children and I have learned to be very patient with them; I simply treat the press as though they were children."

Diana realizes how much the public enjoys seeing her and has learned to pause for a minute when exiting her limousine at a special event so that photographers can take her picture. Anthony Holden, who was once with the *Times,* said, "We had a photographer shooting her for three hours and she wasn't consciously posing—she was just watching the [Wimbledon] match . . . we laid out all fifty photographs . . . There wasn't one that we couldn't have used. She's just amazingly photogenic."

A princess, especially Princess Diana, has very few private moments, and even they, in many instances, have become publicly photographed events. For example, one sunny afternoon, while the princess thought she was privately enjoying the warm air and tropical breezes on a secluded beach in the Bahamas, she was actually becoming the topic of world conversation. This is because a photographer and a writer had crawled on their bellies and hid in the underbush to sneak some snapshots of the pregnant princess in her bikini. Not only was she talked about by millions, but her personal time had become public viewing for the world, as her "bikini" photographs appeared in a number of British and foreign newspapers. We can safely assume that Diana did not consider this a compliment, but instead looked at it as a severe invasion of her privacy.

Much of the public, as well as the royal family, was outraged by the photographs appearing in the papers, and demanded an apology. The next day one of the papers, the *Sun,* printed an apology, but did so by re-running one of the bikini photographs with the caption "Sorry Di."

From the moment Diana became the Princess of Wales, and for the rest of her royal life, she will always be photographed, no matter where she goes or what she does. One frown, one wrong word, and it's tomorrow's headline. She will always be living the life of a goldfish in a glass bowl; people will always be watching her and taking her picture. This is because a great many people in the world are curious about what life is actually like for a real princess. Just about everyone wants to know exactly what she does, where she goes, what she eats, and especially what she wears and how much she spends on her clothes. Some people actually make a business out of "princess

Whenever the Princess of Wales appears in public, she manages to smile, even though she is always hounded by photographers. On occasion they even have invaded her private life. (Courtesy Central Office of Information, London)

The Prince and Princess of Wales pose in front of a tapestry in their Kensington Palace home in London. Prince Charles is wearing a red velvet smoking jacket, which might more appropriately be called a lounging jacket since he does not smoke. The princess is wearing a pink satin outfit. (Courtesy Central Office of Information, London)

watching." They feverishly snap their cameras and try to get as many photographs of the princess as possible because they can be paid anywhere from a few hundred dollars to several thousand dollars just for one snapshot of Diana, depending upon how "shocking" the editors of newspapers and magazines consider the photograph. It has been reported that the photographer who took pictures of the princess in a bikini while she was pregnant received $35,000 from one European weekly for just one of those "bikini" shots.

Photographers will wait hours and hours just for a chance to aim their cameras at Diana. The photographer who took the famous "bikini" shots reported waiting five and a half hours just to get those pictures. Nineteen-year-old Jason Fraser says he waited twenty-seven hours to get a picture of Princess Diana leaving St. Mary's Hospital in London with her newborn second son, Henry.

It's not just the private moments that get destroyed by being photographed and publicized the world over, but even some of the joy found in public moments is robbed from the princess when she becomes hounded by photographers. Most skiers totally enjoy their sport, but for Diana she can no longer completely enjoy it ever again. Too many eyes and cameras are constantly on her and her slightest fall or awkward movement will soon become newspaper headlines. Once, while she was skiing on the Liechtenstein slopes, she was being bothered by press helicopters hovering over her with their telescopic lenses. After trying very hard to be pleasant and patient with them, the princess finally pulled her ski cap down over her forehead and hid her face in her gloves. Prince Charles politely asked her not to do that in hope that the photographers would soon be on their way. Not only did his request become the headlines but the following day the newspapers reported that the princess was "freaking out," and that she was on the verge of a nervous breakdown. The press is not always kind, not even to a princess.

Some days it can be just one photographer who can make himself particularly annoying, as did one on the royal couple's Canadian tour. Sweetly but firmly Diana told him, "You certainly know how to be a pest, don't you?" Luckily that was all the newsman needed to persuade him to leave the princess alone, but not all newspeople are so obliging.

At most public events there are well over two hundred photographers, all trying, with their telephoto-lensed cameras and lightweight, aluminum stepladders, scrambling, to get a picture of the world-famous princess. Some days they're kinder to her than others, but every day has to be a "smiling day" for the princess.

*W*hy do people love Diana so much?

D I A N A is not only one of the best known women in the world but probably one of the most loved also. Her royal position could have easily created a great deal of jealousy, but Diana's glowing personality has turned the public into her world of lasting admirers.

One reason she's so loved is because of her beauty. The Princess of Wales is extremely lovely to look at, and many people are soothed by her peaches-and-cream complexion, warmed by her contagious smile, delighted by her refreshing giggle, and have had their dullest days brightened by the sparkle in her periwinkle blue eyes.

Not only does Diana's beauty provide folks with lots of "looking pleasure," but more importantly her personality supplies them with a distinctive "sharing pleasure" as well. Diana charms people by her natural way of communicating with them. She'll tell them little intimate secrets, and they find her youthful honesty amusing. For example, at her first official meeting, after finding it difficult to sit properly for a very long

Princess Diana visits with Dorothy Gunn at the Washington Home/ Hospice in Washington, D.C. (Courtesy the Washington Home/Lynn Hester)

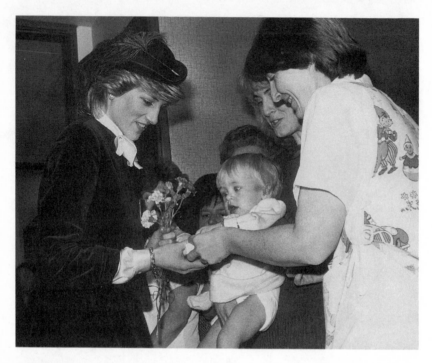

Fourteen-month-old Gemma Sanger presents the princess with a jewelry box made by the children in her ward at the Royal Marsden Hospital of England. Gemma was receiving treatment for a brain tumor. (Courtesy the British Embassy, Washington, D.C.)

time, the Princess of Wales simply confessed, "I've got pins and needles in my bottom."

People love the way she shares her feelings and love the way she shares herself. She has a natural talent for making all those who meet her feel extremely special and very important. That is because she displays a genuine interest and a sincere concern for the people around her. Perhaps Charles's grandmother, the Queen Mother, has helped Diana develop this skill with the advice she had once given the princess, "Forget yesterday and tomorrow when you are meeting people. Today is the most important day and the person to whom you are talking is the most important person."

Diana's sincerity is very evident, as Washington Home and Hospice resident, 102-year-old Mary Bryan, says, "I think she cares about people, the way she talks." Andrea Heid, director of public relations for the home, says, "There were fifty residents in the room and, believe it or not, Diana talked to each and every one of them and had a special comment for each person." Diana makes the "common" person feel she is one of them. She does not allow her royal status to intimidate or frighten others.

Another one of Diana's secrets is that she is a toucher, and people love this. Unlike some royals who discourage physical contact by wearing gloves, as does the queen, or by walking with their hands clasped behind their backs, as does Charles, Diana rarely wears gloves on her walkabouts and will make a special effort to reach far into a crowd to shake as many hands as possible. She treats people as individuals and not nameless faces in a crowd. She'll give people little pats on the shoulder and even a warm, friendly hug. According to royal protocol, commoners are not supposed to touch a princess; but when a child hugs Diana, Diana gives a loving hug in return. She will even bend close to the ground to talk with small children and happily permit them to plant a kiss on her cheek. During her visit to Wales, she held and warmed the hands of one little child who had been standing in the cold rain for hours just to get a glimpse of her. Diana saw another young child crying in the crowd and went over to comfort him. She quickly removed a chocolate bar from her pocketbook and offered it to the youngster, but he was too frightened to accept it. So the princess lovingly tucked it into his small pocket and said, "There you are. Have it later."

It's not just the little ones to whom the Princess of Wales is attracted, but she's interested in and also wants to help as many other people as she can. In 1987, when millions of people across the world feared the deadly disease AIDS (and still do), Diana visited a hospital and shook hands with a patient with AIDS. This not only made the patient feel terrific but sent out an accurate message to the world that the disease is not transmitted by merely touching one another.

Diana even notices little things about people that might go unnoticed by most other royals, and makes a point to let the individuals know she appreciates their efforts. She once complimented a wife for having polished her husband's medal so well that the woman's face beamed as brightly as the medals she had so carefully shined up for the Princess of Wales. No wonder Diana is so loved by so many and is appropriately called "the People's Princess."

People go well out of their way to see her. One Nova Scotian woman, fifty-seven year–old Alice Nicholl, begged for a job to serve as a waitress where Diana would be dining. Alice had never worked as a waitress before but knew this would provide her with the perfect opportunity to see the princess. She was not only correct, but elated afterwards. "It was wonderful!" she boasted.

Sixty-five-year–old Betty Ewing, of the Washington Home and Hospice, summarizes it very simply as "Princess Diana is a very nice lady." But another person at the home, Johnette Clark, adds, "She comes across as much more sincere than one would imagine. There was a sparkle to her. She's bigger than life."

How popular is Diana?

B E F O R E Diana became known as "Charlie's girlfriend," few people, aside from her family and friends, knew her name. When she became engaged to the prince, she gained instant world-celebrity status.

Between the Prince and Princess of Wales, Diana is by far the more popular of the two. It's been reported that ten times as many people come to see Charles when Diana is with him than when he makes an appearance by himself. Obviously, it's Diana and not Charles whom the crowds want to see. Millions of women imitate her hairstyle, for she is one of the most famous and popular women in the world. But no one man ever tries to imitate Charles's hairstyle or manner of dress. The prince certainly realizes his wife's popularity, and frequently walks one or two steps behind her so that all may have a good look at her. He allows her to be the first one to enter a special event because he is well aware of the fact that most of the crowd has come to see his wife and not him. Once, when on a tour of Wales, Charles said he actually became "bowled over" by the extent to which the public adores Diana. Both sides of the streets were lined with people who had waited hours to see the royal couple. When it was decided that they could greet more people if Charles took one side of the street and Diana took the other, all the journalists crossed over to Diana's side, leaving Charles without a single newsperson. One woman on Charles's side of the crowd turned to a friend and said, "Well, we chose the wrong side of the street, didn't we?" Because his wife is now so much more popular than he, people who once knew him simply as Charles, now jokingly call him "Charles, Who?" The same fun-loving people will refer to the royal couple as Diana and "What's His Name?" When the royal couple is spotted by the crowd, screams of "There she is!" will be heard and never "There they are!" One photographer, Kent Gavin, took one hundred pictures at one of the royals's tour. Ninety-two were of Diana, only eight included Charles. The prince said, "I know I'm going to have to get used to the backs of photographers."

One's popularity can also be determined by measuring it against others who are also in the limelight. The London *Sun* photographer Arthur Edwards believes Diana is the world's most gawked-at celebrity and is "bigger than Streisand, bigger than the Beatles." People paid £35,000 (approximately $70,000) each to dine with the royal couple in America. A total of £3 million (about $6 million) was raised for charity during that one night alone. A Palm Beach reporter pointed out "Clint Eastwood, Frank Sinatra, Liz Taylor, and Joan Collins rolled together couldn't reach half that figure."

The degree to which Diana has affected her country's national income (in terms of dollars and cents or in pounds, as in Britain's case) also allows us to measure her level of popularity. Public-relations man Dick Guttman said, "She is also the best advertisement for Britain since the Beatles . . . Princess Diana provides the country with something they couldn't have manufactured." Since Diana has become the Princess of Wales, tourism in Great Britain has skyrocketed. Her favorite restaurants become successes overnight. Every product the princess uses or that people think she uses have been known to instantly sell out. Her plain and simple flat shoes were copied and became so popular that one factory was producing twenty-three thousand pairs a week. Diana has had over one hundred books written about her, which have sold over 27 million copies. Travel experts says Diana's popularity has increased Britain's revenue by well over £7 million, or roughly $14 million. "Dianamania" exists throughout the world, and it doesn't seem to be subsiding even today.

The size of one's welcoming committee also lets the world know the popularity of the guest. When Diana and Charles stepped off their plane at Andrews Air Force Base in Washington, D.C., in 1985, they were met by four thousand admirers, a number much larger than when Charles had visited the U.S. earlier. When the royal couple visited Ottawa, Canada, in 1983, admirers started lining up nine hours before they were scheduled to arrive. Over thirty thousand people waited in 85°F (29°C) weather just to get a glimpse of them. Several people collapsed in the heat and had to be carried off in waiting ambulances.

The number of television viewers also indicates one's popularity. Nine million Britons viewed the royal couple's visit to Australia, while only three million viewed Pope John Paul II's tour of Poland. Over 750 million people across the world witnessed the royal couple's wedding on television. We can safely and accurately state that Diana is truly the world's megastar.

How does Charles feel about Diana's popularity?

CHARLES is extremely proud of his wife's popularity and is not at all insulted that people are more interested in seeing her than they are in seeing him. Charles is delighted that Diana is such a hit with the public, and when large crowds engulf her instead of him, the prince has been known to say, "I'm afraid I've only got one wife. I haven't got enough to go around."

The princess, not the prince, is the one showered with gifts when the royal couple is on tour; and Diana receives so many lovely bouquets from so many caring people that she often turns to her husband for help carrying them. Jokingly, the prince has said, "I'm just a collector of flowers these days." Charles is very supportive of his wife, and from the very beginning has instructed her, "When appearing in public, above all, be yourself. People clearly love you just as you are"; and obviously, so does he.

Although Charles is proud of his wife's popularity, it is easy to see how he could be disappointed when the press writes about his wife's new outfits instead of the important speech he has presented at a special function. Diana certainly agrees with Charles, and she adds, "There is far too much about me in the newspaper, far too much. It horrifies me, when there's more important things, like what goes on in the hospices, or there's been a bomb or something."

Why is Diana called "the Children's Princess"?

DIANA is not only commonly referred to as "the Children's Princess" but has also been called "the Pied Piper of Children." This is because youngsters around the world are attracted to her and she is attracted to them. On Diana's walkabouts she frequently will "coo" over babies and crouch near the ground to talk to little children. Unlike other royals, Diana allows children to give her a hug, and then even hugs them in return. Most children and even adults are thrilled to be touched by a princess. Even the chance to stand next to royalty turns into a lifetime memory for some. Diana once allowed a little boy, who had been blind all his life, to touch her face so he could feel what the princess looked like. He will never forget that moment.

Children of all ages are charmed by Diana's beauty as well

as her loving personality. One student presented her with a bouquet of flowers and told the princess, "I'm afraid your beauty puts the flowers to shame." One three-year-old, Adam Walford, was disappointed that he didn't have flowers to give to the princess, so Diana lowered her bouquet for him to see and lovingly said, "Don't worry, smell these." When a Canadian girl gave the princess three flowers, Diana thoughtfully said, "You shouldn't spend your money on me."

Diana will do her very best not to disappoint children who are expecting her visit. Once, while she was pregnant, she was scheduled to visit 330 children at a primary school in England. So, in spite of a heavy snowstorm, she arrived in time for the children to sing her Christmas carols. Diana once flew in a blizzard because she wanted to comfort a group of mothers whose babies had died of crib death. She said, "I couldn't get there fast enough."

Diana not only goes out of her way for children and their parents, but they also go out of their way just to get a chance to see her. Some children in Australia were driven five hundred miles to see the Princess of Wales. Other youngsters lived farther away and were unable to travel much longer distances, so Diana and Charles thoughtfully appeared on a television show to answer their questions.

It's not just the very young children who find Diana so attractive, but older ones as well. When the princess reached out her hand to accept a single yellow daffodil from eighteen-year-old Nicholas Hardy, he asked, "May I kiss the hand of the future queen?" Diana said, "Yes, you may." After the kiss was given, the princess giggled and added, "You will never live this down."

Children of all ages love Diana. Sixteen-year-old Jonathan Lollar, of Ocean Springs, Mississippi, has been enthralled with her for years. In fact, so much so that his biggest dreams was to one day meet the Princess of Wales. And one November day in 1985 his wish finally came true. It was granted by the

Mississippi chapter of the Make-A-Wish Foundation, which grants wishes to children with life-threatening illnesses. They enabled Jonathan and his mother to fly to Andrews Air Force Base to be the first of the two thousand welcomers to meet Diana and Charles as they began their U.S. visit.

When Jonathan was six years old he developed a brain tumor, which caused him to go blind. But even though he lost his sight, he says he knows exactly what Princess Diana looks like. "Since I've been able to see, I know what colors look like and when something is described to me, I can picture it. . . ." He says, "Diana is like a fast ride on a fast roller coaster. She is breathtaking! She's like something out of a fairy tale. She's just unreal. Diana's just radiant and you can tell she's the type of person that doesn't put on at all. She's just herself. She's a down-to-earth person." Jonathan adds, "Science has said that everyone in the world has a twin but I can assure you there ain't no other Princess Diana." On a scale from 1 to 10, Jonathan rates the princess as "110." "There's no one in the world like her."

Three years after he met her, Jonathan said, "I'm still in orbit." The day was still vivid in his mind. "That morning it was really windy and kind of cold out there at Andrews Air Force Base. But the whole time I was talking to her, I never even thought about the wind. I wasn't cold at all." As the princess held his hand he remembers, "I was just as warm as I could be." Days later Jonathan admitted, "I still haven't washed my palm yet."

Children usually present Diana with flowers, but Jonathan's gift was a gospel record album he had recorded when he was nine years old. He gave this to Diana because he knows she shares his love for music. He says since he lost his sight, his sense of hearing has improved tremendously. "I swear, it's like a radar sometimes, the things I can hear." Jonathan uses people's voice to tell how they look. "My mother tells me I've

By meeting Princess Diana, Jonathan Lollar's wish comes true. He says, "I'm still in orbit." (Photo by Gwendolyn Gentry)   Lady Diana worked as a part-time nanny when she was seventeen years old, and as an assistant at the Young England Kindergarten when she was eighteen. (Courtesy the British Embassy, Washington, D.C.)

Wherever Princess Diana goes, she is showered with flowers. (Courtesy Australian Overseas Information Services)   Princess Diana at the Guards Polo Club in Windsor. (Courtesy Central Office of Information, London)

done well with it so far . . . When you talk to her [Diana] she is very soft-spoken and very kind."

After Jonathan met the princess she went on to the White House to have tea with the president and Mrs. Reagan. Jonathan went on to the "Larry King Show" to share his experience with the television audience, who were able to call up and have their questions answered. Jonathan described his experience as "a tidal wave," and said, "Meeting her was everything I expected." In reality, it turned out to be even more than that, because Diana's attention had turned young Jonathan Lollar into "Mississippi's latest superstar," says columnist Joe Rogers. U.S. Representative Trent Lott called Jonathan "a great ambassador for Mississippi." Senator Kennedy's Deputy Press Secretary later sent Jonathan a letter stating, "Along with the Royal couple, he was the hit of the week." In a newspaper article, Rogers wrote, "Diana, the Princess of Wales, must be a big hit back in England now. After all, she got to meet Jonathan Lollar." Diana's mere presence creates beautiful memories for all the youngsters she meets, and we can be sure she keeps a special spot in her heart for them, also.

Are there people who dislike Diana?

N O one can please everyone all of the time, not even Diana. The Princess of Wales, just like everyone else, has those who are not very fond of her; but in Diana's case, it is believed that more people like than dislike her. But it would not be fair to let those who do not care for her go unnoticed.

Although Charles and Diana are the Prince and Princess of Wales, they spend most of their time in England. In Wales there is a group of nationalistic working people who have never liked nor welcomed royalty to their land. In fact, before Diana and Charles visited the area, some of the Welsh people made signs that said, GO HOME, ENGLISH PRINCESS! Threatening letters had been sent to the British Broadcasting Corporation, (The BBC, as it is commonly called in Britain) and the royal couple was advised, for their own safety, to cancel their visit to Wales. But Diana and Charles carried out their plans and went anyway. Only a few negative incidents happened in Wales. One woman broke through the police barricade and sprayed the royal limousine with white paint. A couple tried to throw a stink bomb at Diana and Charles. But aside from these two incidents, everything else went fine. The newspaper coverage reported that as soon as Diana had arrived she melted the anger of the Welsh people and shortly won over the crowds with her warm, sincere smile and personality. As one reporter put it, ". . . the Welsh have fallen so abjectly and hopelessly in love with Princess Diana."

When the royal couple toured New Zealand and Australia, one angry tattooed member of the Maori tribe, by the name of Te Ringa Mikaka, separated the native grass skirt he was wearing and displayed his bare behind to the royal couple as they passed. Other people protested the royal couple's visit by wearing picket signs and throwing red dye and eggs at the royal's car. But most people were thrilled to see Diana and Charles.

*D*oes *Diana ever make mistakes?*

A L T H O U G H Diana is a princess, she is still human, and, of course, makes mistakes, as does every other human being. The main difference is that when a princess, especially a superstar like Diana, makes a mistake, the whole world instantly knows about it. This means that Diana must try to make her every move a perfect move. But as one can imagine, at first this was not very easy for Diana. One of her first "mistakes" as the Princess of Wales occurred when she was attending the Braemar Highland Games in Scotland. She had been talking with Charles and began to giggle just as the opening measures of the national anthem, "God Save the Queen," began to play. Queen Elizabeth immediately gave the princess such a stern look that Diana instantly replaced her happy face with a more serious one; but Diana's "improper" behavior became a front-page news story.

Other "mistakes" were made further along in Diana's royal career and have been related to the clothes she has worn. Somehow she just can't seem to please all of the people all of the time, but she continues to try. Many have called Diana a "shopaholic" and felt she was spending too much money on her clothes. But when the princess began to "recycle" her clothes on her trip to Italy, she received many complaints because the outfits had been seen before. Diana was then labeled "Secondhand Rose." After she wore the same pink chiffon dress to Milan's La Scala Opera House that she had worn two years earlier, some of the Italians were offended and said her outfits were "inappropriate, dated, and ghastly." The press said the pink chiffon was "too young and foolish" and that her print dress worn for another occasion was "old fashioned and drew yawns." When the princess later wore a cream satin suit with a bowtie she was then criticized for wearing an "Italian waiter suit." Even London's daily *Sun* criticized the clothes Diana wore in Italy. They called her emerald-green checked coat "bizarre."

When the Prince and Princess of Wales were on tour of Australia, Diana's wardrobe was again criticized as being "an insult to the people of Australia," and fashion writers labeled her "Dowdy Di." They said the princess was "saving the best for America."

Although Diana makes mistakes, she does learn from them. She constantly tries to please the public, and if they do not like a dress she has worn, she will not wear it again unless it undergoes major changes.

Diana's "mistakes" have not been limited to her giggles and clothes but have also spilled over into her eating patterns. When she and Charles were on their tour of Italy, some Italians complained that she was drinking orange juice instead of the Italian wine of which they are most proud. Many also thought that she should have been eating more pasta.

There's a story that's been told in London about another of Diana's "mistakes." The princess was the guest of honor at a small private luncheon and as usual didn't eat very much. In fact, it's been said that the guests had barely begun to eat their meals when Diana "picked at her food for only a few minutes and then placed her knife and fork together on her plate." This usually signifies one is finished eating, and if anyone else had done this, it would not have created a problem. But when the Princess of Wales does it, a major problem results. Protocol, or royal etiquette, says that it is improper for anyone to continue eating after royalty has stopped. So all the guests instantly stopped eating their sumptuous meal, which they had barely begun, and had their plates whisked away by waiters. Diana learned a very important lesson that day, and it is a mistake she will not repeat.

*D*oes Diana drive a car?

WHEN Diana was seventeen years old, she enrolled in a driving school. She failed her test for a driver's license the first time but passed it the second. For a while she drove her mother's Renault 5 and then "Mummy" gave her a new Volkswagen. Diana unfortunately crashed it.

Shortly after her eighteenth birthday Diana received a red Mini-Metro car from her father, but often rode her bicycle through the crowded streets of London. But this quickly stopped when she became known as Charles's girlfriend, because she was always being followed by photographers and newspaper reporters.

When Diana became a princess she drove a 1984 bulletproof blue Ford Escort and later a $32,000 Ford Sierra. She also has the use of a $56,000 Jaguar and a $170,000 Bentley Turbo R. When the princess drives she is usually accompanied by a private detective for security reasons. Prince Charles had been driving an Aston Martin, a Ford Granada, and then a Jaguar Sovereign XJ6. In 1987 Diana received a new, dark blue Jaguar XJS. Little William "drives" a miniature electric toy Jaguar, which looks just like that of his parents. He received this $40,000 toy from the manufacturer who made his parents' car.

Does Diana work?

BEFORE Diana became engaged to Prince Charles she had a few different jobs. While she attended the West Heath School she worked and played with youngsters in a home for the handicapped. At another time she assisted an elderly woman with shopping and household chores. Diana also had a few part-time nanny positions. At seventeen Diana tried teaching young children to dance, but soon realized that job wasn't what she had expected. At eighteen she became an assistant at the Young England Kindergarten, which was a position she enjoyed tremendously.

Once Diana became engaged to Prince Charles, she stopped working at the kindergarten and started attending to the many different tasks involved with her wedding and her new princess-to-be position. Once she became the Princess of Wales she soon was known as a "working princess." This is because Diana spends a great deal of time visiting and lending her support to various schools, hospitals, and community centers. Diana does this because she knows her visits cheer up people, and she says, "I think people like to see people being happy if possible. . . ." Her presence at these organizations helps individuals forget their problems, at least for a little while. It also draws attention to their situation and encourages the more fortunate to make contributions to these needy causes.

One of Diana's special interest groups is the British Lung Association. Diana is particularly concerned with their work because her father suffers from lung disease. The Princess of Wales is also interested in helping the blind and the deaf. For a time she was learning sign language and said, "Well, I'm trying, but I think it's important to show that you're interested and you're not just breezing in and out, having seen them for a morning. I've got all my senses and they haven't and I'm learning how they adapt, or if they've been deaf and dumb since birth how they cope and how they deal with the outside world that doesn't always want to know about them."

Diana also supports associations for the elderly and for the prevention of childhood diseases. She aids the Red Cross and colleges for physicians and surgeons. She is a patron or president of twenty-nine British charities.

Diana's concerns go beyond the medical field and include organizations for the performing arts. She sponsors a number of music and dance programs for both children and adults. In-between these programs she finds time to participate in ceremonial tree plantings, ship christenings, and factory openings. She also makes a special effort to promote the buying of British goods. In 1985 she and Charles visited the U.S. to help draw attention to the $50 million worth of British merchandise being sold by the J. C. Penney store in Springfield, Virginia. Charles said, "Creating a positive atmosphere toward Britain is one of the major functions of the royals. I would like to hope that through trying to engender that sort of awareness and interest . . . that other things will follow, like increased trade and export opportunities."

Diana, as the other English royals, has no political power, but serves her country simply as a figurehead. Diana takes her position as princess very seriously and continually lives out the Prince of Wales's motto "Ich Dien," which means, "I serve."

She attends between three and four hundred events each year to help focus attention on needy and important causes. With 365 days to a year that averages out to approximately one public function each day. But Diana will sometimes attend a number of events in one day, keeping her weekends free to spend with her family. In 1985, while Diana and Charles visited Washington, D.C., they took part in fourteen events within three days. Within six days, in 1986, Diana made twenty-five public appearances in Canada, and then continued with Charles on to Japan, where they attended twenty-nine functions in five days. In spite of the large number of functions she attends, Diana never looks tired. Perhaps this is because she is frequently reminded of Queen Mary's famous words, "You are a member of the British royal family and *we* are never tired."

Diana not only draws attention to people and organizations with special needs and functions, but her royal visits also create interest in a country's striking tourist attractions. Her well-publicized 1983 photograph in front of Australia's flat-topped Ayers Rock brought this sacred aborigine landmark to the world's attention. Wherever Diana is, the world soon learns about it. The Princess of Wales can rightfully be labeled a "teaching princess" as well as a "working princess."

How many servants help Diana?

DIANA'S household staff is made up of approximately forty

people. Highgrove is staffed with a cook, a housekeeper, three maids, a butler, and three footmen. Some of these people also work at Diana's Kensington Palace home. If Diana and Charles are planning a large gathering, they "borrow" help from the queen's Buckingham Palace staff and pay them for the evening. There are hundreds of other people who help manage Diana's public engagement schedule. There are those, such as her personal detectives and bodyguards, who accompany the princess whenever she is in public. When on tour in Canada, Diana was escorted by a woman karate expert of the Mounted Police unit, who was dressed plainclothes. Diana also has two dressers whose full-time job it is to maintain her clothes. They also keep records of when and where the princess has worn each outfit. Diana has three part-time ladies-in-waiting and one senior, full-time lady-in-waiting, Anne Beckwith-Smith, who has been with the princess since 1981. Anne walks a little behind Diana during all public appearances and helps the princess in whatever way she can. She'll stand guard outside the bathroom, or the "loo" as the British call it, whenever Diana needs to use it. Anne will carry extra bouquets of flowers when necessary and keeps a supply of "emergency" items in her pocketbook in case Diana needs them, such as a sewing kit, an umbrella, tissues, make-up, safety pins, a spare pair of panty hose, spot-removal tissues, and also an extra copy of the speech Diana will be making.

Diana certainly appreciates Anne's help and friendship. After the royal couple's Australian tour, Diana gave Anne a pair of diamond and sapphire gold earrings with the message: "I couldn't have done it without you."

Some women are very jealous of the fact that Diana has so much "household help." One Australian woman, Jill Shoebridge, who had a young son at the time, told Diana, "I wish I had a nanny just like yours to look after my son." Diana responded instantly, "I would swap with you anytime. I wish I didn't have to leave William to his nanny. I would rather do what you are doing." At first Jill felt Diana "must be mad." Later she realized the extreme pressures on a princess and changed her attitude, ". . . it is an awful lot to have a baby as well as doing the things she had to do . . . I don't envy her royal life style at all . . . I still get to see my baby every day. I feel sorry for her," states Jill.

How does Princess Diana feel about being a mother?

D I A N A and Charles, or "Mummy" and "Papa," are proud parents of two sons, William and Henry. Both parents believe that bringing up their children is one of their most important jobs.

The royal couple's first child, William, is heir to the throne, which means that after Charles he will become the King of England. William was born June 21, 1982, and weighed seven and a half pounds. His birth made Diana Britain's youngest royal mother in more than one hundred years. It took one week before his parents publicly announced his name: Prince William Arthur Philip Louis. During this week he was unofficially called "Baby Wales" by the press. Since he's been such a lively youngster, Diana has called him "my mini-tornado." The parents of his nursery school playmates dubbed him "Billy Basher." Charles calls him "Willie the Wombat," and both parents frequently call him "Wills."

Prince William was not only their first child but first in many other ways as well. He was the first royal baby to be born in a hospital instead of the palace. He was born in St. Mary's, which was the same hospital in which Sir Alexander Fleming discovered penicillin. William was the first heir to the throne to have his father present while being born. Charles, feeling proud of both himself and his newborn son, said, "It's a very grown-up thing . . . He looks marvelous, fair, sort of blondish. He's not bad," and he "has the good fortune not to look like me." As William grew older he was the first royal youngster to attend school outside the palace. All other royal children have been educated by tutors at home for their beginning school years. It was very important to both Diana and Charles that William was educated "outside," because they did not want him to grow up shy and insecure by not being around other youngsters, as had been the case when Charles was young.

When Prince William was born, thousands of people waited at the hospital in the drizzling rain for sixteen hours just to hear the announcement of his birth and be among the first to see him leave for home. The queen ordered two, forty-one gun salutes to be fired in his honor. When Prince Charles was born, he had received only one, forty-one gun salute, but the queen did have the church bells ring five-thousand times as a special tribute to her first son. The world shared in the royal family's rejoicing at William's birth. Well-wishers sent him over four-thousand two hundred toys. Diana kept some of them for William but donated the rest to her favorite children's charity. The nation also shared in hearing William's first word spoken on TV, "Yuk," which was one of his mother's common expressions.

Diana and Charles's second son, Henry, was born September 15, 1984, and weighed six pounds four ounces. Unlike his brother, his name was announced immediately: Prince Henry Charles Albert David, or just plain Harry for short. When Diana compares both boys she says, William "pushes himself right into it. Harry is quieter and just watches." Both boys attended nursery schools, which have installed bulletproof windows for the royal children's protection and also keep a detective or two standing near by.

Diana and Charles want to spend as much time with their

The royal family christening group: HRH the Princess of Wales with her son Prince William of Wales are seated at center, with HM Queen Elizabeth II at left and HRH Princess Anne seated behind the queen. To the right is HM the Queen Mother, with Diana's mother, Mrs. Frances Shand-Kydd, seated behind her. Standing, from left to right, are Capt. Mark Phillips, HRH the Duke of Edinburgh, Mr. Angus Ogilvy, Queen Anne Marie, Princess Alexandra, King Constantine, Lady Susan Hussey, HRH the Prince of Wales, Lord Romsey, the Duchess of Westminster, Earl Spencer, Ruth Lady Fermoy, Sir Laurans van der Post, and HRH Prince Edward. (Courtesy Central Office of Information, London)

Prince Charles and Princess Diana with their children: Prince William, the future King of England, and infant Prince Henry. (Courtesy Central Office of Information, London)

sons as they can because they want their children to know and feel comfortable with their parents. There's a popular story told about Charles's attitude toward his mother when he was growing up. It's said that when he was five years old he hadn't seen his mother for six months because she was away on a royal tour. When she returned it's believed that Charles had almost forgotten who she was, because when they met again he politely shook her hand and quickly went back to the comfort and security of holding his grandmother's hand. Diana and Charles don't ever want a situation like this to happen to their children, so they spend as much time with them as possible. As royal parents they also know that when Charles assumes more responsibilities when (and if) he becomes king, there will be less time to spend with the children.

Diana does a lot for her sons. She'll change diapers and arrange her plans so that she does not have any official duties before ten in the morning. This way she will have ample time to give the boys breakfast and even frequently take them to school. She tries to have lunch with them whenever she can and makes a special effort to be with them at bath and bedtime. Charles is also very much involved with his sons. In fact so much so that once in order to get William used to taking a bath he actually climbed into the tub with his young son. Both Diana and Charles love to read bedtime stories to the boys. "It's terribly important that parents should do this," says Diana. She believes that she, not their nanny, should be the one kissing them good night.

Because Diana's parents were divorced and Charles's parents traveled a lot without him, both Diana and Charles want to provide their own children with the happy, close-knit family-life they did not have as children. Diana especially wants her children with her as much as possible. In 1983, before Harry was born, Diana and Charles toured Australia. Although most royals advised her against it, Diana refused to leave young William at home and brought him along on tour instead. He instantly became the hit of their trip. When she must be on tour without her children, she calls them frequently by telephone, which is equipped with a scrambler (a device that scrambles signals unless one has a special receiver) so eavesdroppers would not be able to understand their conversation.

When Diana or Charles are not able to care for their sons, nannies Ruth Wallace and Olga Powell assume this responsibility. But Diana has made it clear that they are only mother's helper and not mother's stand-in.

Diana wants the boys' nannies to be as informal as possible. She requested that they wear everyday clothing instead of the customary uniform. Diana also has the boys call the nannies by their first names and does not permit the women or any other palace help to bow or curtsy to young Prince William and Prince Harry. She does not want her children to be subject of "baby worship." She has set these standards because she wants her children to be raised as close as possible to be like other "normal kids." She is well aware that her children will soon be burdened with many royal responsibilities. When William was on their Australian tour he was just an infant and, of course, held in his parents' arms. But someone complained that the feet of this little royal never touched the Australian soil. Diana responded, "Goodness, he isn't the pope, you know."

Diana tries to create a balance between normalcy and nobility for her sons. During the Christmas holiday of 1987 she waited in line with them for fifteen minutes at a London department store so they could see Santa Claus just like other families. She could have easily used her royal status to go to the head of the line, but instead she insisted that her sons wait on line like everybody else. She's even taken them to a public movie theater and afterward for hamburgers at an American-style restaurant.

Neither parent hits or spanks their children and neither do the nannies. Barbara Barnes, their first nanny, had two rules:

Diana is holding three-year-old Prince Henry's hand as he is about to attend his first day of kindergarten. Prince William attended the same school two years earlier. (Courtesy Central Office of Information, London)

Tea at the White House with President and Mrs. Reagan. Diana is wearing red, the president's favorite color (and hers, too). (Photo by Mary Anne Fackelman, the White House)

she never smacks a child and doesn't raise her voice in anger."
As both Diana and Charles agree, raising children so they will
be "happy and secure" is one of their most important jobs.
Charles adds, ". . . one of the most important roles any woman
could ever perform is to be a mother." With an enormous
smile Diana says, "It's amazing how much happiness a small
child brings to people."

*W*hen will Diana become Queen?

I N order for Diana to become the Queen of England, Charles,
of course, must first become king. This would mean he would
then, as his mother does now, reign over the United Kingdom
as well as be the Head of State for nearly fifty more countries
in the Commonwealth (which is a community of nations previously under British Sovereignty). Crowning Charles as king
can occur by one of two ways. First, unfortunately, would be
by the death of his mother, Queen Elizabeth II; the second,
by the queen abdicating, or giving up, her role. Both are very
unlikely to happen for quite some time for the queen is in
very good health and has no intention of abdicating her throne
at this time. She has a strong sense of duty to her country and
a great love and concern for Charles and his family. She well
remembers how her own royal duties interfered with her role
as parent and does not want to put Charles in this same conflicting position any sooner than necessary. She wants him to
have as happy a family life as possible, especially while his
children are very young. The queen feels there will be time
enough after her grandchildren are older for Charles to assume
the many duties required of a king.

When Charles finally does become king, Diana would not
just automatically become queen. Charles will have to decide
whether he wants her to remain a princess or wants to crown

her as his queen. Charles is certainly well aware of the fact that the world is anxiously awaiting the time when Diana will become queen. If and when that time arrives, Diana would become "queen consort." This means that she would not be the ruling monarch but just the wife of the reigning king. If she had become queen through birth and not marriage, Diana would have become "queen regnant," or ruling queen. Either way, in reality, neither she nor Charles nor even Queen Elizabeth II have "ruling power" over Great Britain. Since 1688 Parliament has been the ruling body. The queen simply "reigns" but does not "rule."

What is the "proper" way to greet the Princess of Wales?

M A N Y people who have been taught to bow before a king or queen do not know how to properly greet a princess. In fact, thousands of Americans were asking this exact question prior to the royal couple's visit to the United States. So the British embassy conveniently issued a card stating, "Americans do not curtsy or bow, but an incline of the head would be very polite."

As people began to "brush up" on other royal etiquette, they learned that one does not speak to a royal first but instead waits to be spoken to. One does not touch a royal nor extend a handshake unless the royal offers a hand first. But Diana has been known to "bend" these rules when she is among young people. She seems eager to meet them and will frequently share hugs and kisses.

Best of luck if you should ever have the good fortune to meet her. After having read this book, you will certainly be well enough informed to carry on an interesting conversation with her. If you are not lucky enough to chat with her for any length of time but only have a moment to present her with a bouquet of flowers, remember to attach a card with your name and address, for you will surely receive a thank-you note as a lifetime remembrance from the Princess of Wales, Diana.

The Royal Highnesses, the Prince and Princess of Wales. (Courtesy Central Office of Information, London)

B   Nesnick, Victoria
DIA   Gilvary.

        Princess Diana

$13.45

DATE			